W9-ACN-937

COUNTRY STUDIES

JAPAN

Michael Witherick

Series Editor: John Hopkin

Heinemann Library
Chicago, Illinois

Reed Educational & Professional Publishing
Published by Heinemann Library,
an imprint of Reed Educational & Professional Publishing,
100 N. LaSalle, Suite 1010
Chicago, IL 60602
Customer Service 888-454-2279
Visit our website at www.heinemannlibrary.com

Typeset and illustrated by Hardlines
Printed in Hong Kong

05 04 03 02 01
10 9 8 7 6 5 4 3 2 1

Library of Congress Cataloging-in-Publication Data
Witherick, M. E.
    Japan / Michael Witherick.
        p. cm. -- (Country studies)
    Includes index.
    ISBN 1-57572-422-7 (Library binding)
    1. Japan--Juvenile literature. [1. Japan.] I. Title. II. Country studies (Des Plaines, Ill.)

DS806 .W56 2000
952--dc21
                                        00-033512

Acknowledgments
The publishers would like to thank the following for permission to reproduce copyright material:
Maps and extracts: papan Map Centre, Tokyo, Japan; p. 20B extract from "Promises and tears mingle with Japan's settling dust," by Kevin Rafferty, in *The Guardian*, 21 January 1995.
Photos: Science Photo Library, p. 4A, 40A; Michael Witherick, pp. 6A, 7C, 32B; Panos Pictures, pp. 9C, 15C, 24B, 56B; PA News, p. 13C; Nigel Hicks, p. 15B; Environmental Images, p. 17B; Axiom Photographic Agency, p. 18A; Spectrum, p. 19B, 43C, 43D; SYGMA, p. 20A; Corbis, pp. 22A (top), 22A (bottom), 35C; Eye Ubiquitous, pp. 25C, 53C; The Kansai Electric Power Company, p. 31C; Seagaia Ocean Dome Complex, p. 33C; Robert Harding, pp.34A, 37D; Geoff Howard, p. 41D; Cephas, p. 46B; Kansai Airport, p. 47D; Tony Stone, p.48B; Japan National Tourist Organization, pp. 49D, 49E; Panasonic, p.54A; Robert Harding, p. 56A; Still Pictures, p. 57C.

Cover: background, Panos Pictures/Jim Holmes; foreground, Robert Harding Picture Library.

Every effort has been made to contact copyright holders of any material reproduced in this book. Any omissions will be rectified in subsequent printings if notice is given to the publisher.

· Some words are shown in bold, **like this.** You can find out what they mean by looking in the glossary.

Contents

1 INTRODUCING JAPAN

A Nation of Islands

▶ **Where is Japan located?**
▶ **What are its main physical features?**

Japan is an island nation located 125 mi. (200 km) off the east coast of Asia and separated from it by the Sea of Japan. Japan is also a nation of islands. There are four main islands and about 3,900 others forming an **archipelago**.

The Japanese archipelago stretches over more than 20 degrees of latitude. In the north, the island of Hokkaido reaches almost as far as Sakhalin, a part of Russia. In the south, the Ryukyu Islands reach almost to Taiwan.

Plate margins and island arcs
Japan is located on a very unstable part of the earth's surface where three **tectonic plates**

meet—see map **C**. Along the **plate boundary** are **fold mountains** and **island arcs.** For example, the Bonin Islands Arc has been formed where the Pacific Plate and Philippine Plate rub against each other. These two plates are dragged under the Eurasian Plate—diagram **D**. This causes the earth's crust to be pushed up into a series of fold mountains. Mountains form the backbones of the four main islands. Because of the movement of these three plates, volcanoes and earthquakes are an important part of Japan's geography.

A This satellite image shows Japan and the Asian coast.

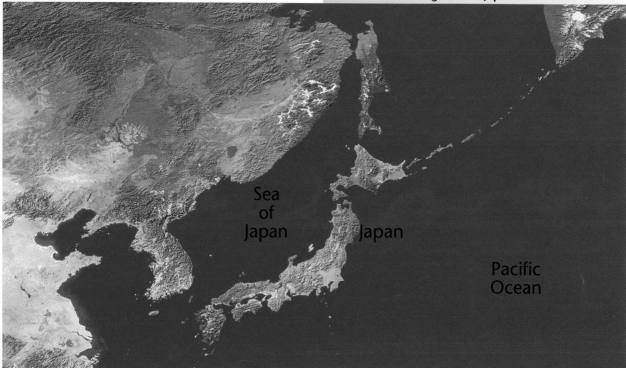

Sea
of
Japan

Japan

Pacific
Ocean

	No. of islands	Share of land area (%)	Share of population (%)	Share of GDP (%)
Hokkaido	263	22.1	4.6	3.8
Honshu	1,546	61.1	80.3	84.4
Shikoku	472	5.0	3.4	2.6
Kyushu	1,641	11.8	11.7	9.2
Total	3,922	145,883 square mi.	126.2 million	$1,022 billion

B Japan's main islands

C Arcs, islands, and neighbors

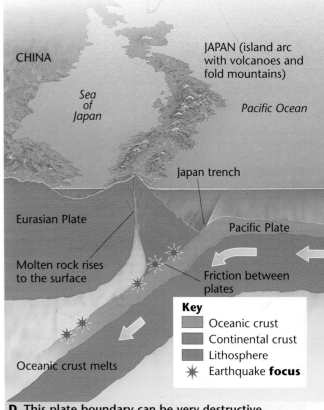

D This plate boundary can be very destructive.

FACT FILE

Naming the country

The Japanese refer to their country as *Nippon*. It means "the place from where the sun rises." This description was first used in a letter sent to China by a seventh-century Japanese prince. He wanted to describe the location of the lands that he ruled. Even to this day, Japan is known as the land of the rising sun. The national flag, the *Nisshoki*, shows a red sun. Japanese people are called *Nihonjin*. Outsiders and foreigners are called *gaijin*.

The origin of the name *Japan* is much less certain. One possibility is that it came from the word *Yatpun*, the name used by people in southern China to describe the islands that are now Japan. Early Dutch traders and settlers were the first to call the islands Japan.

▶ **How has Japan's history influenced its economy?**

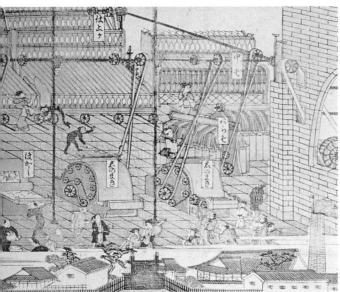

A This artwork depicts the modernization of Japan.

Isolation and national unity

Some of the answers to Japan's success today can be found in the past. For more than 200 years, Japan was isolated from the rest of the world. Japan's rulers, the *shoguns*, believed this was the best way to keep Japan from becoming a colony of a country in Europe. But by the middle of the nineteenth century, it was obvious that Japan was falling behind Europe and the United States in technology, weapons, and wealth.

Modernization and expansion

In 1867, a revolution caused important changes.

- The emperor replaced the *shogun* as leader of all Japan.
- Japan opened up to foreigners, new ideas, and technology.
- New industries were set up, especially the making of weapons.
- New roads and railways were built.
- The education system was improved.

These changes were successful, but they brought more problems. The growing industries needed more raw materials and energy than the country had. The population grew, but Japanese farmers could not supply the people with enough food. So Japan began invading its neighbors, starting with Taiwan, Korea, Manchuria, and parts of China. This aggression, along with the bombing of U.S. naval forces at Pearl Harbor, Hawaii, drew Japan into conflict with the United States and its allies during the Second World War and caused the war to spread to the Pacific.

Defeat and reconstruction

The Second World War was a disaster for Japan. In 1945, Japan surrendered after the allies dropped atomic bombs on the industrial city of Hiroshima and the port of Nagasaki. Much of the country was in ruins, and the people were

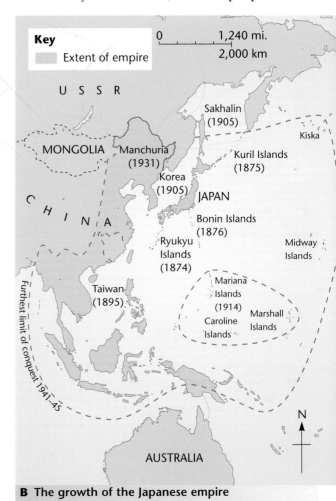

Key

Extent of empire

0   1,240 mi.
2,000 km

U S S R

Sakhalin (1905)

Kiska

MONGOLIA   Manchuria (1931)

Kuril Islands (1875)

Korea (1905)

JAPAN

C H I N A

Bonin Islands (1876)

Ryukyu Islands (1874)

Midway Islands

Mariana Islands (1914)

Taiwan (1895)

Caroline Islands

Marshall Islands

Furthest limit of conquest 1941–45

N

AUSTRALIA

B The growth of the Japanese empire

C The town of Kashima was one of many that grew rapidly during the 1960s.

badly depressed. Japan had lost **face**. Little changed for five years, but in 1950, **communist** China and North Korea invaded South Korea. The United States realized Japan might be the next country to fall to the communists. It was better to have Japan as an ally rather than an enemy. With American help, Japan was on the road to recovery.

The economic miracle

From 1955, the economy grew quickly. Heavy industries like iron and steel, shipbuilding and petrochemicals prospered. Consumer industries made a growing range of products, such as electrical goods, cars, and cameras. By 1968, Japan had become the world's second most powerful economy—a ranking it has kept ever since. This period of fast growth is often called the "economic miracle."

The oil crises and low growth

In 1973 and 1979, the price of crude oil skyrocketed. Unfortunately for Japan, its heavy industries were thirsty for oil. About three-quarters of Japan's energy came from oil, so Japan had to rethink its economy. Since 1973, the economy has grown much more slowly. But Japan has kept its place as a **superpower** by making some important changes.

- It uses energy from more sources.
- Energy is used more efficiently.
- Heavy industry has been slimmed down.
- **High-tech** industries have grown.

Most worrying for Japan in the late 1990s is competition from other industrial countries, especially the "Asian Tigers"—South Korea, Taiwan, Singapore, and Hong Kong, which is now part of China.

FACT FILE

The birth of a nation

In the first century, Japan was a collection of more than 100 small, independent kingdoms scattered over the four main islands. By the fourth century, one of these kingdoms had grown so powerful, it dominated the western half of Honshu, the northern half of Kyushu, and all of Shikoku. The family that ruled it became the imperial family. The emperor today, Emperor Akihito, is a direct descendant.

In the eighth century, the power of the emperor began to weaken. Powerful families became feudal lords, or *daimyo,* over large areas of land

with many peasants. These *daimyo* grabbed much of the land and made great fortunes. The families in their turn were overthrown by a warrior class, or *samurai,* which the feudal lords had created to keep their peasants under control. The rule of the warrior class through their leaders, the *shoguns,* lasted nearly 700 years, coming to an end in 1867. Early in the seventeenth century, the ruling *shogun* broke off all relations with foreign countries, expelled foreigners, and refused to allow foreign travel. In the years of isolation that followed, Japan became a unified nation.

Japan and the Asian Pacific Region

▶ Why is the Asian Pacific region so successful?

A The Asian Pacific region

Leading a dynamic region

The Asian Pacific region is made up of the thirteen East Asian countries that face the Pacific Ocean, plus Hong Kong, China. Japan has had the most economic success so far, but other countries are quickly catching up. Today, the region produces about a quarter of all the world's economic wealth. It is quickly becoming the center of the global economy and is estimated to have about half of the world's population.

Why is the region doing so well? It is partly because:
- the countries are eager to enjoy better living standards
- they see Japan as a shining example they can follow

- among them they have raw materials, energy, and plenty of low-paid workers
- they can produce goods that are in demand at competitive prices.

The Asian Pacific countries can be divided into four groups—by color on the map—based on their wealth. The difference between the wealthiest and poorest countries is huge—see table **B** where the colors match the map.

Low-income countries

The low-income countries are all **communist** countries. Their economies work differently than the **market**, or **capitalist economies** of the other ten countries. Things are beginning to change in all of these countries, especially China. China is an "awakening giant," with its huge population and rich natural resources.

Lower-middle-income countries

The lower-middle-income countries all have economic growth and rising living standards. Manufacturing industry is behind much of this growth. These countries have plenty of natural resources. Three of them are nations of islands, so building good transportation links is a major challenge. Thailand does not have this problem, and farming and tourism are more important there than in the other three.

Higher-middle-income countries

In the higher-middle-income countries, manufacturing industry has been booming for more than 25 years. All these countries are small in area and in population. Another name for them is the "Asian Tigers." In 1997, Hong Kong was handed back to China, and it remains to be seen whether this will continue to be a dynamic area under its new ownership. Brunei is a special member of this group. It is one of the richest countries in the world. It is a big oil producer, with a tiny population and little industry.

Economies	Ranking	GDP per person(U.S.$)	GDP (U.S.$billion)
High income	1 Japan	36,863	4,509.9
Higher middle income	2 Singapore	24,024	68.9
	3 Hong Kong	21,752	131.8
	4 Brunei	17,611	4.6
	5 Taiwan	11,415	241.2
	6 South Korea	8,616	379.6
Lower middle income	7 Malaysia	3,668	70.6
	8 Thailand	2,131	124.9
	9 Philippines	973	63.9
	10 Indonesia	765	144.7
Low income	11 Vietnam	579	38.3
	12 North Korea	553*	12.7
	13 China	353	413.7
*estimates	14 Cambodia	94	0.9

B Asian Pacific countries, plus Hong Kong: a league table of economic growth and wealth (1992)

C Some think Singapore today is a model state.

High-income countries

At the moment, Japan is the only high-income country in the region, with the highest wealth per person. It also has by far the biggest economy. China is its nearest rival.

The Asian Pacific region will likely become even more powerful and influential in the twenty-first century. For the time being, Japan will remain the superstar. But all these countries need to remember that economic success also has its costs.

FACT FILE

The Asian Tigers

Hong Kong, Singapore, South Korea, and Taiwan are known as the "Tigers." They are called this because of their high rates of economic growth and the speed at which they are catching up with Japan. All are small in area and have high **population densities**, or people per square mile. Manufacturing industry has been important in their economic growth. Because of lower labor costs, business has gradually been taken from Japanese firms. For example, South Korea and Taiwan have been doing well in shipbuilding, textiles, and electrical goods. Hong Kong and Singapore now compete with Tokyo as major financial centers.

	Average annual growth in GDP (1990–94) (%)	Population density (1992) (per square mi.)	Employment in secondary sector (1995) (%)	Employment in tertiary sector (1995) (%)	Average income (1995) (U.S. $)
Hong Kong	5.2	14,196	35	64	17,860
Singapore	8.3	14,126	35	65	19,310
South Korea	7.6	1,234	36	47	7,670
Taiwan	6.5	1,591	39	50	11,000
Japan	2.1	865	34	60	31,450

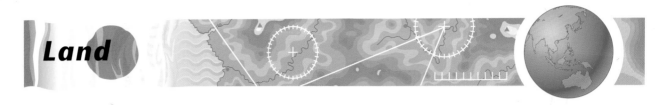

2 THE PHYSICAL ENVIRONMENT

Land

> ▶ Why is space a scarce resource in Japan?
> ▶ How has Japan tried to overcome this?

A shortage of space

Japan has a big problem: three-quarters of its land area is mountainous and of no use for settlement. Less than a fifth of the country is lowland, but the population and economic activity are concentrated there. Usable space is a scarce resource in Japan.

Lowland Japan

The shortage of space is made worse because Japan's lowland is broken up into many small plains. Most of these plains are located along the coast and are cut off from each other by uplands. Linking the lowlands together by road and rail has been very expensive, but Japan's transportation engineers have become very good at building tunnels and bridges. The island of Shikoku, with the smallest amount of lowland, poses some of the worst transportation difficulties. The biggest lowland is the Kanto Plain, on Honshu. The two largest cities in Japan, Tokyo and Yokohama, are located there.

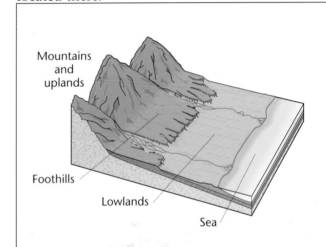

Mountains and uplands

Foothills

Lowlands

Sea

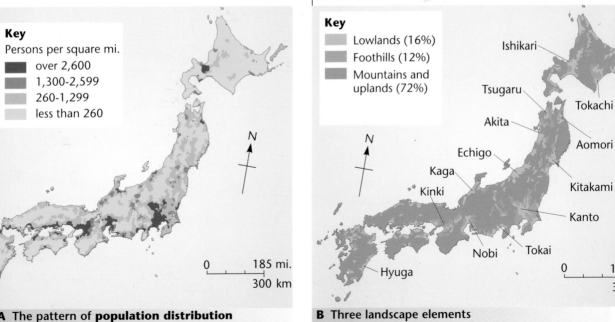

Key

Persons per square mi.

- over 2,600
- 1,300-2,599
- 260-1,299
- less than 260

N

0   185 mi.

300 km

Key

- Lowlands (16%)
- Foothills (12%)
- Mountains and uplands (72%)

Ishikari

Tsugaru

Tokachi

Akita

Echigo

Aomori

Kaga

Kitakami

Kinki

Kanto

N

Nobi   Tokai

Hyuga

0   18⁵

30⁰

A The pattern of **population distribution**

B Three landscape elements

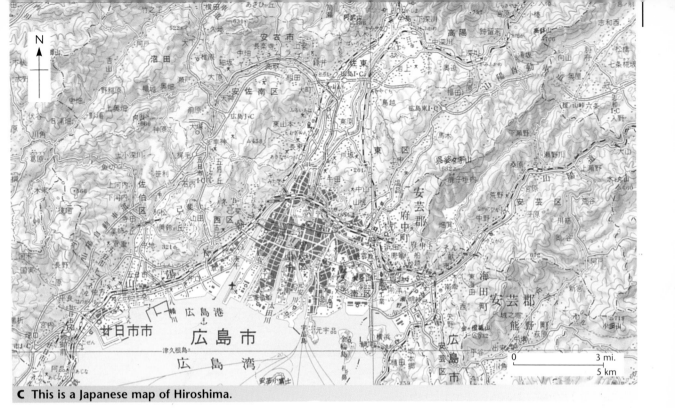

C This is a Japanese map of Hiroshima.

Upland Japan

Mount Fuji (12,388 ft./3,776 m) is Japan's highest mountain. There are fourteen others over 9,800 ft. (3,000 m); most of them are old volcanoes. They are part of the Hida Mountain chain that runs the length of Honshu along a boundary between three **tectonic plates.**

The rest of the uplands are not so high, but they are cut into by deep, narrow valleys with steep sides and thin soils. These features make transportation links difficult and the land not much good for farming. The main value of the uplands is their forests. The uplands also offer people opportunities for leisure—peace and quiet, hiking, climbing, and winter sports.

Between the lowlands and uplands are the foothills. Although the soils are not very fertile, they are used for farming because land is scarce.

FACT FILE

Highest mountains

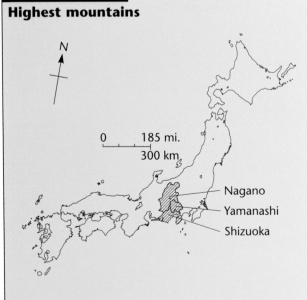

Mountain	Location (prefecture)	Height (ft.)	Height (m)
Fuji	Shizuoka	12,388	3,776
Kita	Yamanashi	10,472	3,192
Hotaka	Nagano	10,466	3,180
Aino	Shizuoka	10,463	3,189
Yariga	Nagano	10,433	3,180
Azuma	Shizuoka	10,305	3,141

Slope of land (% of land area)					
3° and less	8°	15°	20°		30° and over
14%	15%	24%	16%	23%	8%

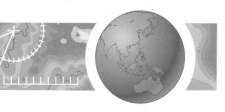

Climate

▶ **What are the features of Japan's climate?**
▶ **How does the climate affect people?**

Climatic contrasts

Japan's islands stretch over 20 degrees of latitude, so there are big differences in climate between the north and south. There are three types of climates in Japan.

- Hokkaido has a **continental climate** with cool summers.
- Northern Honshu has a continental climate with warm summers.
- Southern Honshu, Shikoku, and Kyushu have a **humid subtropical climate.**

A climate of six seasons

Japan's climate varies from season to season, as well as from place to place. There are six seasons (diagram **B**). The two rainy seasons,

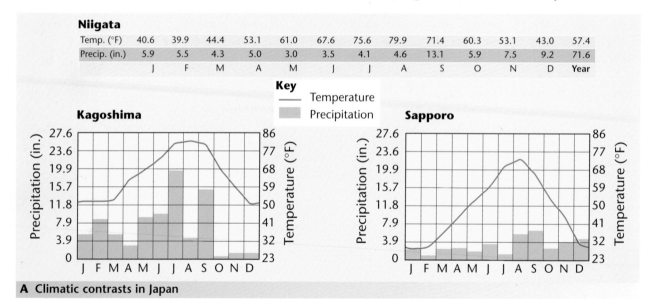

Niigata	J	F	M	A	M	J	J	A	S	O	N	D	Year
Temp. (°F)	40.6	39.9	44.4	53.1	61.0	67.6	75.6	79.9	71.4	60.3	53.1	43.0	57.4
Precip. (in.)	5.9	5.5	4.3	5.0	3.0	3.5	4.1	4.6	13.1	5.9	7.5	9.2	71.6

A Climatic contrasts in Japan

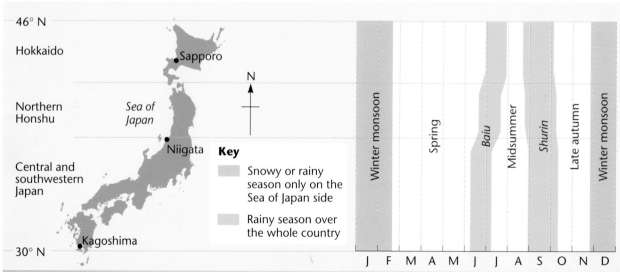

B The six seasons

C It is very difficult to battle the strong winds of a typhoon.

when the **polar front** passes over Japan, are called *baiu* and *shurin*. The length of the hot, humid midsummer ranges from two months in the south to half that in the north. The winter monsoon is a season marked by bitterly cold northwesterly winds that blow from high pressure in Siberia and bring rain and snow.

The good news for farming

Temperature and rainfall are important to farming. Rice is the main food in Japan, so levels of heat and moisture must be right for this crop. Rice will grow on the lowlands over most of the country; in fact, in the south, there can be two crops a year. Because the climate is so varied, a range of other crops can be grown across the country.

Tourism

The climate of Japan is a resource that is useful for tourism.
- Winter skiing is very popular in the mountains of Honshu and Hokkaido.
- The tropical climate of Kyushu and Okinawa is popular for sunshine breaks in summer and winter.

The downside

The Japanese climate is not all good news. Snow is a problem in winter in the north and on high ground, making transportation difficult. Melting snow and the heavy rains of the two wet seasons cause flooding. **Typhoons** track towards Japan between July and November, bringing torrential rain and strong winds. They are one of Japan's worst **natural hazards.**

FACT FILE

Natural vegetation

Forests are of great importance in Japan. They cover about 65 percent of the land. After such a long history of human use, there is very little untouched or virgin forest left. Wood is still widely used for:
- building houses
- fuel
- making paper, furniture, and plywood.

There are three main types of forests:
- the coniferous forests of northern and eastern Hokkaido
- the cool, temperate deciduous forests extending from southern Hokkaido to central Honshu, and also on the high mountains of southern Japan
- the subtropical evergreen forests of southern Honshu, Shikoku, and Kyushu.

For the cool, temperate deciduous forests and the subtropical evergreen forests, the original vegetation is being replaced by more useful and faster-growing cedars, cypresses, and pines.

Land use	% of area
Arable	11
Forest and woodland	67
Permenant Crops	1
Permenant Pasture	2
Other	19

Water and Coasts

▶ **Why are Japan's rivers both a useful resource and a hazard?**
▶ **Why is the coast important to Japan's economy?**

Japan's rivers

Japan's rivers drain into either the Pacific Ocean or the Sea of Japan. Because no place in Japan is very far from the sea, rivers are short. The longest river, the Shinano, is only 228 mi. (367 km) long.

In the mountains, rivers flow fast in deep valleys. In the lowlands, the rivers become wide and shallow. Many rivers have built high banks, called **levees**, which raise the river channel above the level of the lowland. This helps farmers, who can drain water off to **irrigate** their rice fields. But if the river banks break, there is a risk of flooding.

The risk of flooding is worsened after heavy rain, perhaps caused by a **typhoon**, or when the snow melts suddenly in spring. Surface runoff reaches upland rivers quickly because of the steep slopes, so rivers rise quickly. This fast reaction shows in the sharp **hydrograph** of the Sendai River. To reduce the risk of flooding, gates have been built to hold back flood waters. In the lowlands, levees have been raised even higher.

Lakes

Japan's uplands contain many small lakes, often in the craters of old volcanoes. Some are used as reservoirs to supply water to factories and homes. Others are used to generate **hydroelectric power (HEP).** Many, like the lakes around Mount Fuji, have become tourist attractions. They offer beautiful scenery and opportunities for water sports.

The coast

Since Japan is an **archipelago**, it has a very long coastline. The coastline is made even longer by many small headlands and bays. This coast has created some important opportunities for the Japanese.
• Japan's sheltered bays have provided good locations for ports.
• Coastal shipping has helped link up settlements along the coast.
• Fishing has always been an important source of food and work for the Japanese.

Once the coastal waters were rich in fish, but overfishing has reduced stocks dramatically. Fish now comes mainly from international seas or from fish farms.

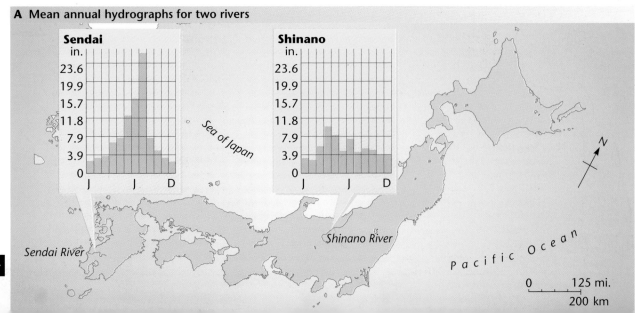

A Mean annual hydrographs for two rivers

LAKE BIWA

Lake Biwa

By far the biggest lake is Lake Biwa. In the past, it was famous for its beauty. Unfortunately, its location close to the cities of Kyoto and Osaka has led to conflict over its use. It is heavily used by people for leisure, but it is also used as a source of water. It has shrunk in size and become polluted by sewage and industrial waste.

B Many people enjoy visiting Lake Biwa.

THE INLAND SEA

C These workers are farming seaweed.

The Inland Sea separates the islands of Shikoku, Honshu, and Kyushu. Because its waters provided fish and shelter for shipping, and its shores provided lowland for settlement and farming, this area was settled early in Japanese history. Since then, some coastal settlements have become major port cities, like Hiroshima, Kurashiki, and Ehime. The coast provides good anchorages for today's huge supertankers bringing oil and industrial raw materials. Land **reclamation** created the extra space needed for new large-scale industries. Today, fish farms in the waters of the Inland Sea produce fish, shellfish, and seaweed—all important foods in Japan. But industrial pollution is a problem.

FACT FILE

Rivers and lakes
Major rivers

	Location (prefectures)	River basin area (square mi.)	Length (mi.)
Tone	Gumma, Chiba	6,502	200
Ishikari	Hokkaido	5,575	167
Shinano	Nagano, Niigata	5,595	228
Kitakami	Iwate, Miyagi	3,919	155
Kiso	Nagano, Aichi	3,514	141
Tokachi	Hokkaido	3,479	97

Major lakes

	Location (prefectures)	Surface area (square mi.)	maximum depth (mi.)
Biwa	Shiga	258.9	64.5
Kasumigaura	Ibaraki	64.7	4.5
Saroma	Hokkaido	58.1	12.2
Inawashiro	Fukushima	39.9	58.1
Nakaumi	Shimane, Tottori	33.5	10.6
Kussharo	Hokkaido	30.7	9.3

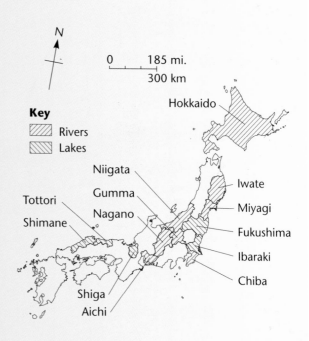

N

0   185 mi.
       300 km

Key
- Rivers
- Lakes

Hokkaido

Niigata
Gumma
Tottori
Shimane
Nagano

Iwate
Miyagi
Fukushima
Ibaraki
Chiba

Shiga
Aichi

Natural Hazards

▶ What makes Japan's environment hazardous?

A dangerous environment

A **natural hazard** is a natural event that threatens damage and destruction. Japan is quite a dangerous part of the earth, with a range of natural hazards. What matters to people is how often and where hazards occur, how much damage they can cause, and what can be done to avoid this damage.

Volcanoes and earthquakes

A number of hazards occur because Japan is located on an unstable part of the earth's crust, where three **tectonic plates** meet. Japan has about one-tenth of the world's active volcanoes. Volcanic activity is going on all the time somewhere in Japan, but most of it is not violent. More worrying are the volcanoes that lie **dormant** for hundreds of years and then suddenly come to life. Mount Fuji is a volcano thought to be extinct, but who can be certain?

Earthquakes are frequent in Japan. Many places have as many as 100 in a year. Most of these are weak, but some are very destructive. Earthquakes often set off other hazards, especially landslides and **tsunamis**. Tsunamis are huge tidal waves caused by earthquake tremors stirring the sea. They cause flooding and death in the coastal lowlands.

Typhoons

Between three and thirty **typhoons** a year strike Japan between July and November. These revolving tropical storms bring very high winds, sometimes up to 125 miles per hour (200 kilometers per hour), causing enormous damage. Torrential rain falls, often 12 in. (300 mm) in 24 hours, causing floods and landslides.

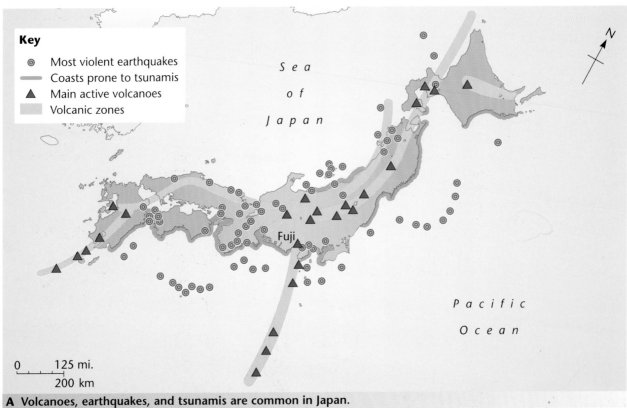

Key

- ◎ Most violent earthquakes
- ▬ Coasts prone to tsunamis
- ▲ Main active volcanoes
- ▢ Volcanic zones

Sea of Japan

Pacific Ocean

Fuji

0   125 mi.

200 km

A Volcanoes, earthquakes, and tsunamis are common in Japan.

B The heavy rain of a typhoon caused this landslide.

Floods

Floods are also caused by heavy rain in the two wet seasons and by melting winter snow. They are made worse by the steep gradients of the rivers, which descend suddenly onto coastal plains and cause a lot of damage because the plains are often heavily populated.

Landslides

Landslides are the most frequent and widespread of Japan's natural hazards. Once heavy rain soaks into loose soil or rock on steep slopes, this material can easily slip downhill, slowly or with a sudden rush.

Landslides are often set off by earthquakes or by people's activities, such as clearing slopes of vegetation.

Counting the cost

The Japanese live in a very hazardous environment. They can do little to reduce the number or frequency of natural hazards. Their only choice is to try to reduce the risk of death and serious damage as much as possible by being aware of the dangers and making careful use of the land.

Table C gives some idea of the amount of damage caused by natural disasters in a typical year. Except when there is a major earthquake, death and injuries are fairly low.

People –	killed	95
	injured	425
Buildings –	ruined	1,397
	flooded	102,438
Roads –	places destroyed	2,565
Bridges –	swept away	107
Railways –	places damaged	141
Communications broken		107,993
Boats –	sunk	326
	damaged	174
Rice fields – swept away		5,146
People affected		95,907
Total cost of damage		$5.84 billion

C Hazard damage in 1990

FACT FILE

Hazards caused by people

Not all environmental hazards are linked to natural events. Serious hazards can be caused by human activities. Fire, road accidents, and war are three examples. Pollution is another, but in this case, the physical environment, including air and water, is affected. Japan has suffered a great deal of environmental pollution. It was worst during the 1960s when the country was at the peak of its "economic miracle." People's health was badly affected.

The table shows that the levels of some air pollutants have been cut. However, nitrogen dioxide is still on the increase. The major cause is the continuing increase in the number of motor vehicles on Japan's roads.

Air pollution	1965	1991
Sulphur dioxide (ppm)	0.057	0.011
Carbon monoxide (ppm)	6.0	2.2
Nitrogen dioxide (ppm)	0.022	0.029
Suspended dust particles (mg per cubic foot)	0.0014	0.0011

ppm = parts per million

The Environmental Balance Sheet

A The city of Nagano on Honshu is an example of lowland congestion.

The physical environment can have powerful influences on people, both positive and negative. It gives people opportunities, but also sets limits on what they can do. By looking at the difficulties and opportunities for Japan in this chapter, we can draw up an environmental balance sheet.

Environmental difficulties

The Japanese face four main environmental difficulties.

- Japan's mountains and uplands make transportation difficult.
- There is very little space for agriculture and settlement.
- Japan has a harsh climate in the north and in the mountains, particularly in winter.
- There are many **natural hazards**.

There are two other important problems. First, Japan has few minerals, such as iron ore, and few energy resources, such as oil. So it is all the more remarkable that it has become a leading industrial nation. Second, Japan's soils are not very fertile. Even on the lowlands, the soil needs careful handling and frequent treatment with fertilizers.

Environmental opportunities

However, Japan's physical environment has been encouraging to people in various ways.

- The sheltered bays and inlets of the coast provide good sites for ports.
- The coastal waters once produced plenty of fish.
- The climate is good for growing rice and other crops.

- The climate is good for different types of tourism.
- The spectacular mountain scenery is attractive to tourists, including hikers, climbers, and winter sports enthusiasts.

Two other resources have been useful. First, Japan's forests have supplied the country with building timber, fuel, and paper for centuries. Second, Japan has many hot springs close to volcanoes. Taking a hot spring bath has always been a popular form of recreation, so many small resorts have grown up around hot springs, especially in the mountains of Honshu and Kyushu.

B Many Japanese enjoy hot spring baths.

The environmental balance

You might think that Japanese people have to live in an unfriendly environment, with a shortage of space and frequent natural hazards. But there are also some plus points that may balance things out.

We can be more certain that the physical environment has had a big influence on Japan's development. Japanese people have made the most of their environmental opportunities and made adjustments for the difficulties. But we need also to remember that people often make competing demands on the environment. For example, there is conflict between farming and urban growth on the lowlands, and between forestry and golf course development in the uplands.

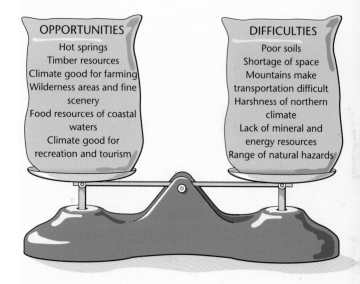

OPPORTUNITIES	DIFFICULTIES
Hot springs	Poor soils
Timber resources	Shortage of space
Climate good for farming	Mountains make transportation difficult
Wilderness areas and fine scenery	Harshness of northern climate
Food resources of coastal waters	Lack of mineral and energy resources
Climate good for recreation and tourism	Range of natural hazards

C Japan's environment has pluses and minuses.

FACT FILE

Mineral resources

Japan does have some minerals, but the problem is that there is not enough of each mineral, and they are not of a high enough quality. Local coal and iron ore were mined for the iron and steel industry in the nineteenth century. The more **accessible** and richer deposits have been depleted. Today, it is much cheaper to **import** supplies. Copper, lead, zinc, chromium silver, and gold are still being mined, but in all cases output is declining and imports are increasing. Deposits of uranium are proving useful in supplying fuel for the country's nuclear power stations. The lack of oil and natural gas is probably the most serious shortage.

Since 1955, the number of people employed in mining has fallen from over 400,000 to a mere 25,000. Nearly half of today's Japanese miners are working with nonmetallic minerals, such as clays, limestone, sand, and gravel.

The Kobe Earthquake

▶ **What was the impact of the Kobe earthquake?**

▶ **What lessons were learned?**

A The city of Kobe suffered terrible destruction.

Kobe is the sixth-largest city in Japan and is one of the world's largest ports. At dawn on January 17, 1995, Kobe was rocked by a series of earthquake tremors. The worst of these reached 7.2 on the **Richter scale**. In a matter of minutes, Kobe had become a disaster area.

Images of tilted expressways, collapsed buildings, rescuers digging in the rubble for survivors, and bewildered people salvaging belongings from ruined homes were soon seen on TV around the world. It was Japan's worst earthquake in 72 years. The final toll was nearly 6,000 people dead, 26,000 injured, and 310,000 homeless. About 75,000 buildings were damaged or destroyed, with a repair bill estimated at $95 billion.

Two lessons were quickly learned in Kobe:
* The emergency services reacted too slowly and had great difficulty coping with the disaster.
* People suffered deep trauma, even many who were not physically injured.

A tearful young woman and her husband returned to their destroyed home. Unsteadily they climbed over the debris to the remains of what had been their first-floor bedroom with the futon still spread on the floor. The woman stooped to retrieve a grimy favourite handbag that she saw peeping out of the dirt, then bowed her head and said a final prayer "of thanks to God for helping us out alive, of sadness that the family home has been utterly destroyed and for help—to recover and start again."

She bowed again, stepped back, scrambled down and let a demolition worker swing his bulldozer to flatten what was once home. Her husband put a finger behind his glasses to wipe away a tear. They had not the heart to remove clothes washed overnight in the machine that mockingly seemed to have escaped unscathed.

"It was our family home and had belonged to my husband's father," the woman explained.
"I don't know where we are going to get the money to build a new one or where we will stay in the meantime, especially if our companies do not start work again. We are five, including two young children and my husband's elderly mother, so it will be hard to cope."

From "Promises and tears mingle with Japan's settling dust" by Kevin Rafferty in *The Guardian*, January 21, 1995

B This is a personal account of an earthquake victim.

Since Kobe, Japan has begun a thorough review of the whole earthquake issue. Three questions are being asked. They relate to the way people react to a **natural hazard**.
- Is the earthquake hazard being taken seriously enough—hazard perception?
- Is the risk of earthquake damage being underestimated—risk assessment?
- Is the right sort of action being taken to reduce the risk of serious damage—risk reduction?

The Kobe earthquake suggests that the answer to all these questions is no. The major problem is the costs of actions such as:
- quakeproofing buildings and **public services**
- building sea walls to protect coastal settlements from **tsunamis**
- setting up emergency services
- educating people on what to do when an earthquake strikes.

It is a matter of balancing the costs of these actions against the risk of a strong earthquake occurring. Clearly, there are limits to how much money can be spent on antiearthquake

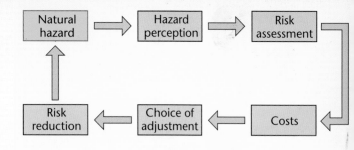

C People react to natural hazards in stages.

measures. But sometimes there will be earthquakes so strong that they destroy even the most advanced forms of quakeproofing.

The basic problem with earthquakes is that we cannot forecast exactly when or where they will occur and with what strength. The Japanese had been expecting a big earthquake to strike one of their major cities. But architects and engineers believed that by using modern technology they were making new buildings, transportation lines, and public services reasonably quakeproof. A few minutes of earth tremors in January 1995 shattered that belief. The clear message from Kobe is that more has to be done to cut the damage threatened by a major earthquake.

FACT FILE

Earthquake name	Date	Magnitude	Deaths	Damaged houses
Great Kanto	09/01/23	8.3	142,807	576,262
Tanazawa Range	01/15/24	7.3	19	1,298
North Tango	03/07/27	7.3	2,925	16,295
North Isu	11/26/30	7.3	272	2,240
Sanriku offshore	03/03/33	8.9	3,008	7,479
Tottori	09/10/43	7.2	1,083	7,736
Tonankai	12/07/44	7.9	998	29,189
Mikawa	03/11/45	6.8	1,961	12,142
Nankai	01/13/46	8.0	1,432	15,640
Fukui	06/28/48	7.3	5,390	39,111
Chile earthquake tsunami	05/23/60	8.7	139	2,830
Niigata	06/16/64	7.5	26	2,250
Tokachi offshore	05/16/68	7.9	52	691
Miyagi offshore	06/12/78	7.4	28	1,383
Sea of Japan	05/26/83	7.7	81	1,584
SW Hokkaido offshore	07/12/93	7.7	234	3,557
Kobe	01/17/95	7.2	6,000	75,000

3 THE ECONOMY

Postwar Growth

▶ How has Japan become an economic superstar?

The second half of the twentieth century has been a remarkable time for Japan. In 1950, it still lay in ruins after the destruction of the Second World War. The people were in poor health and had lost the will to succeed; defeat had meant a serious loss of **face.**

Today, Japan is the world's second wealthiest nation, after the United States. Its businesses and products are found all over the world. Japanese people are seen as hard workers, big spenders, and lovers of the latest gadgets and fashions.

Explaining the economic miracle

So how has Japan become a world superstar? The answer lies in the growth of the Japanese economy. Three important changes have taken place since 1950:

1   Japan's economy has grown enormously. It has slowed down recently, but is still growing faster than those of rival countries.

1945–55	9.1%
1955–65	10.0%
1965–75	8.3%
1975–85	4.2%
1985–95	3.3%

B Average annual rates of economic growth

2   There have been changes in the balance of **primary**, **secondary**, and **tertiary** activities that make up the economy.

3   In the past 25 years, many of Japan's industries and businesses have set up factories and offices in other countries. More and more of Japan's wealth is being created offshore, or outside the country.

Human resources

Japan has few resources of raw materials or energy. But Japan's human resources are very good at producing goods and services. Japanese people have:
• a high standard of education
• a healthy attitude toward hard work
• a willingness to try new ideas
• a desire to be part of a team
• a wish for Japan to succeed as a country.

A Tokyo in 1945 and 1995: Japan has changed.

Management and organization
The way Japanese businesses are run has also helped the economy, especially by:
- using new technology and production methods
- cooperation between employers and workers
- cooperation between giant companies and many small family firms
- cooperation between the government and business.

MITI

The Ministry of International Trade and Industry could be Japan's "secret weapon." For more than 40 years, it has collected and analyzed information from around the world on new products, new technology, new markets, and new competition. The results are passed on to Japanese industries and businesses to help them to decide on new products and services to develop. In the U.K. and the United States, businesses have to do this sort of research for themselves.

a) % Total employment

	Primary sector	Secondary sector	Tertiary sector
1960	30.2	28.0	41.8
1970	17.4	35.2	47.4
1980	10.4	34.9	54.7
1990	6.0	33.9	60.1

b) % GDP

	Primary sector	Secondary sector	Tertiary sector
1960	12.6	39.0	48.4
1970	5.9	43.1	51.0
1980	3.5	38.6	57.9
1990	2.8	38.4	58.8

C Japan's employment structure is changing.

FACT FILE

Government intervention
Although Japan is considered to be a **capitalist** country, the running of the economy has not been left entirely to market forces. In fact, the economy has been carefully managed. The government has frequently stepped in to help steer the growth of the economy. This intervention includes

- protecting Japanese agriculture from foreign competition
- promoting **high-tech** industry
- persuading manufacturing to move to less congested locations outside the Pacific Belt
- managing the value of the Japanese yen in order to keep Japanese goods from becoming too expensive for foreign buyers
- controlling **imports**
- keeping the demand for goods and services at a steady level.

Japan is not the only one to protect its agriculture.

Farming and the Rural Economy

▶ **How is farming in Japan changing?**
▶ **What is the impact on rural communities?**

A shrinking sector

Only six percent of Japanese jobs are now in the **primary sector:** farming, fishing, forestry, and mining. They create only three percent of the country's wealth. Farming is the most important of these jobs.

Rice production

Japan now grows over three-quarters of all the rice it needs. New strains of rice, heavy use of fertilizers, and mechanization give much higher yields than in the past, and the crops can now be grown even on Hokkaido with its cold climate. The main rice-growing area is in northern Honshu. However, two harvests a year are possible in the warm south.

Meeting changing demands

Japan's varied climate allows a range of cereals and fruit to be grown. On Hokkaido, cattle are kept for meat and milk, and barley is grown for beer and whiskey. In the south of Japan, Kyushu and Okinawa grow subtropical fruits like mandarin oranges and pineapples. All this produce is in greater demand because the Japanese diet and tastes are changing. People are eating less fish, soy, and rice. Beer has replaced *sake* as the most popular alcoholic drink.

	1965	1990
Farm households	5,665,000	3,835,000
Full–time farmers	1,219,000	592,000
Part–time farmers	4,446,000	3,243,000
Farms under 1.24 acres (%)	38	42
Rice (1,000 tons)	12,409	10,347
Soya beans (1,000 tons)	230	272
Milk (1,000 tons)	3,221	8,059
Pigs	3,976,000	11,817,000
Beef cattle	1,886,000	2,703,000
Fertilizers (% production costs)	13	7
Machinery (% production costs)	14	31
Labor (% production costs)	56	37

A Agricultural changes (1965–90)

Today, Japan produces about 60 percent of the food it needs, in spite of problems with Japanese farming. Table **A** gives some information about the difficulties. Government support is needed to keep many farmers in business. **Subsidies** are given to help meet the costs of fertilizers, machinery, and improvement projects.

FARMING ON THE KANTO PLAIN

The Kanto Plain is Japan's largest lowland. It has an urban population of over 25 million, centered in Tokyo and Yokohama. Large areas of farmland have been swallowed up by urban growth. The farmers who are left can make quite a good living by supplying the cities. Wealthy city people will pay good prices for fresh fruit and vegetables, milk, eggs, and flowers. More and more sales are being made at the farm gates.

B These farm crops are sold to an urban market.

PART-TIME FARMING

The Koga family's farm is near Matsuyama on Shikoku. It is an intensive **arable** farm of only 3.7 acres (1.5 hectares). The farm has been in the family for generations; Isao took over the farm when his father died thirteen years ago. Before then, he worked as a joiner in Matsuyama and helped with the farm on weekends.

Isao quickly found he was earning less than before and not enough to support the family. He lacked the cash to buy extra land from neighbors. After two years, he went back to his old job. His wife and mother now do most of the farm work. Isao and his children help out in their free time.

Two-thirds of the land is used to grow rice and barley (both supported by government subsidies). The other third is used for vegetables, including eggplants and onions, and fruits like tomatoes. All the produce is sold in Matsuyama or to urban markets in southern Honshu, thanks to the opening of one of the bridge links between Shikoku and Honshu.

Apart from the inputs already mentioned, others include fertilizers and herbicides, a rotary digger, and a mechanized watering system. The Kogas are also members of a local **cooperative**. This provides bulk buying and selling facilities as well as advice.

Today, Japan has half a million full-time farmers and three million part-timers. Most of these, like Isao Koga, earn more from other jobs. Unfortunately, part-time jobs are not enough to keep people in rural areas. Communities are slowly dying as people move to the cities for work. Without government subsidies, many more farms would be abandoned altogether.

C The Koga family's farm produces many crops.

FACT FILE

The Japanese diet
Rice has always been the main food, eaten along with vegetables, fish, and *miso,* a mixture of fermented soybeans, barley, and rice. Pickles, some of them very strong, are a popular accompaniment. For centuries, the eating of meat was forbidden because the people's religion, Buddhism, did not allow it.

Since the end of the Second World War, there have been important changes in what the Japanese eat. Bread has become part of the diet. There has been a great increase in different kinds of meat, particularly beef and chicken, and dairy products. Western-style fast-foods have also caught on, especially with younger people. Most Japanese cities now have their branches of McDonald's, Dunkin' Donuts, Pizza Hut, and so on.

Some of the Japanese dishes liked best by foreign visitors are

- sushi—small balls of specially prepared cold rice topped with slices of raw fish, shellfish, seaweed, and sometimes a type of omelet. Top sushi chefs are highly sought after.

- tempura—a fritterlike dish of fish, shellfish, and vegetables dipped in a light batter and deep-fried in vegetable oil.

- sukiyaki—slices of beef braised together with vegetables in a small amount of liquid seasoned with soy sauce and other ingredients.

Manufacturing

▶ How is industry in Japan changing?

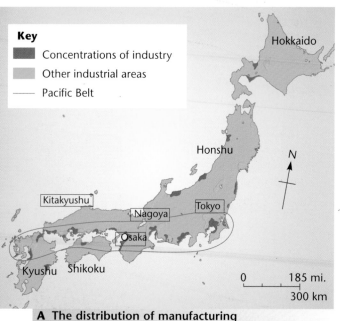

A The distribution of manufacturing

Key
- Concentrations of industry
- Other industrial areas
- Pacific Belt

Hokkaido
Honshu
Kitakyushu
Nagoya
Tokyo
Osaka
Kyushu Shikoku

0   185 mi.
         300 km

Manufacturing industry has been an important part of Japan's economic miracle. But today, manufacturing creates less than 40 percent of Japan's wealth and only one-third of the jobs.

Industrial changes

Between 1950 and 1973, heavy industries like iron and steel, shipbuilding, and petrochemicals were the most important. These industries **imported** large amounts of raw materials and energy. The **oil crises** in 1973 and 1979 made these much more expensive, so product prices rose, and Japan's heavy industries became less competitive. Japan had to restructure its industry by building up other types of manufacturing.

Two types of industry have helped to make up for the decline in heavy industry. Consumer industries make a wide range of products, from cars to camcorders, pianos to personal stereos, for people in Japan and abroad. The other type of manufacturing is **high-tech** industry.

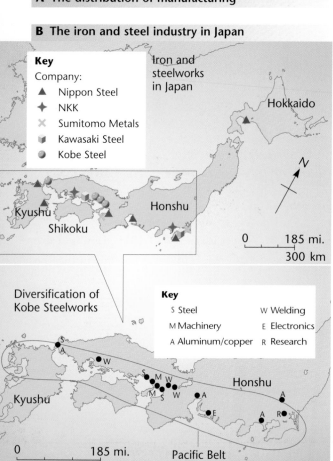

B The iron and steel industry in Japan

Key
Company:
- ▲ Nippon Steel
- ✦ NKK
- ✕ Sumitomo Metals
- Kawasaki Steel
- Kobe Steel

Iron and steelworks in Japan

Hokkaido
Kyushu
Shikoku
Honshu

0   185 mi.
         300 km

Diversification of Kobe Steelworks

Key
- S Steel
- M Machinery
- A Aluminum/copper
- W Welding
- E Electronics
- R Research

Kyushu
Honshu

0   185 mi.
         300 km

Pacific Belt

KOBE STEEL, LTD.

Kobe Steel was formed in 1905. Its location in a major port city was useful for importing iron ore and coal. The company expanded in the 1950s and 1960s and set up new smelting works elsewhere in Japan. But in the 1970s, foreign competition and falling demand forced the company to make important changes:
- It closed small uneconomic steelworks.
- It concentrated steel production in a few large works.
- It diversified by converting factories for other things, such as engineering.

In the 1980s and 1990s, the company has diversified even more. It has businesses in information technology, robotics, and **biotechnology.** It has also set up around 30 **branch plants** in other countries. These changes have helped Kobe Steel, Ltd. to survive and prosper in a rapidly changing world.

Distribution

About 70 percent of Japan's industries are located in the Pacific Belt. They are close to the main markets for their products in the big cities, and the main ports for **exporting** products overseas are nearby. This helps businesses because it is easy to move products between factories. But there are also costs. Land is more expensive and wages higher, and there is more traffic congestion and pollution in the industrial areas.

YAMAHA MOTOR COMPANY

Honda, Kawasaki, Suzuki, and Yamaha produce most of the world's motorcycles. They sell over a million new machines each year in Japan alone. Narrow city roads and traffic congestion make motorcycles a popular form of transportation.

The Yamaha Motor Company was set up in 1955 at Hamamatsu, an area with plenty of skilled workers. Today, it produces nearly two million motorcycles a year, most being sold overseas. Two important changes have taken place. First, the company now makes a range of products, including all-terrain vehicles, go-karts, power boats, and outboard motors. Second, it has set up branch plants, or factories, in other countries, especially in Southeast Asia and South America.

Number of workers in Japan		11,200
Number of factories		10
% share of motorcycle sales in Japan		30
% output	motorcycles	50
	marine products	21
	power products	11
	car engines	8
	others	10
% total output exported		59
Overseas branch factories	Asia	6
	South America	4
	Europe	3
	Africa	1

C Yamaha Company statistics

FACT FILE

Craft industries

The Meiji Restoration after the *shoguns* in 1867 marked Japan's beginning as a modern industrial nation. That is not to say that Japan had no industries before that. In fact, there was a whole range of what are called "craft industries." These relied heavily on the manual skills of workers and generally used only small amounts of raw materials. Perhaps the most widespread craft industries were:

- silk—a natural fiber made by silkworms that is woven into a fabric mainly used in expensive clothing

- ceramics—pottery and porcelain made from local clays and decorated by skilled artists

- lacquerware—household and decorative objects coated by the thick sap of the lacquer tree, making them resistant to water and corrosion

- swords—originally made as weapons, but later becoming treasured as works of art.

In the middle of the nineteenth century, when Japan began to open its doors to foreigners, there was great interest in some of the products of the craft industries, particularly silk, ceramics, and lacquerware. These were important exports for Japan, even up to the beginning of the Second World War.

▶ Why are high-tech industries good for Japan?
▶ What is the tertiary sector, and why has it expanded so much?

High-tech industries

An important part of Japan's **high-tech** industry is making machines, such as computers and satellites that collect and process information. Another is using new methods to make new materials and drugs. These industries are good for Japan because they use small amounts of raw materials and energy. They help keep Japanese industry more efficient and its products ahead of competitors, such as with robotics. High-tech industries need a lot of well-educated and skilled workers, especially for research and development. So they are important in helping Japan to restructure its industry.

Service industries

The **tertiary sector** is the part of Japan's economy that has grown most since 1950. It has grown as people have become wealthier, because as people earn more, they can spend more on services. The tertiary sector, or service industries, can be roughly divided into two groups: commercial, or profit-making, and social, or nonprofit-making.

Today, about 26 million people in Japan work in profit-making service industries. These include:
• retailing and wholesaling
• transport, communications, and information industries
• business and finance
• tourism.

The nonprofit-making services, or social services, provide for people's welfare. For example, more than three million people are employed in the fields of medical care and education.

A further ten million people work in the government and other services.

	Japan	U.S.	Germany	Italy	France	U.K.
Robots in use, 1995	377,025	66,286	51,375	22,963	13,276	8,314
Robots for every 10,000 workers, 1994	245	31	51	45	30	17

A World robot production and use, 1994–95

TECHNOPOLIS PROJECTS

There are more than 40 new towns being built in Japan as technopolis projects. Each project has three parts:

• an industrial area of high-tech factories and support services

• a university

• a housing area for workers and their families.

The site chosen for a technopolis should be within 30 minutes of a major city, and should be well-connected in terms of national and international transportation networks.

The government supports these projects because it wants to keep Japan's position as a world leader in high-tech industry. It wants each prefecture to have a technopolis project, so all parts of the country are involved in high-tech industry.

MATSUSHITA CORPORATION

Matsushita is one of Japan's major transnational companies. It has research and development bases in Japan, Singapore, Taiwan, the U.S., Germany, and the U.K., and business bases in more than 40 countries, mostly in Southeast Asia, North America, and Europe. It makes electrical and electronic goods such as:

- home appliances, such as microwave ovens and refrigerators
- video and audio, such as new wide-screen TVs
- telephone products, such as mobile phones and fax machines
- electronics, such as semiconductors and CD–ROM drives.

Matsushita is best known for its Panasonic audio-visual products, like the camcorders made at its Osaka factory. They are assembled there from components, many of which are made by small family businesses.

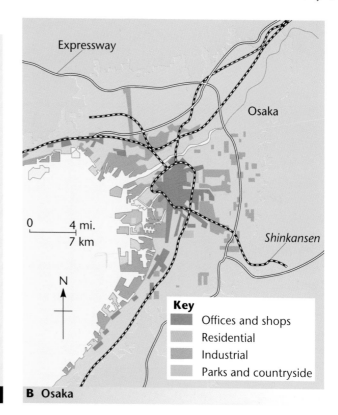

B Osaka

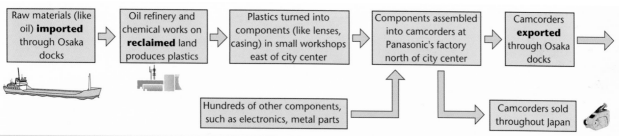

C Panasonic camcorder production requires many detailed steps.

FACT FILE

Social services

All employers and workers in Japan have to contribute on a regular basis to insurance plans that will pay for pensions and medical care. They are free to choose between plans run directly by the government and those run by private companies.

Most other social services are paid for by national and local government through the tax system. These services include help for the unemployed and those on very low incomes, as well as support for families with more than three children.

Most important of all, though, is education. Education is free for the years of compulsory schooling, that is, between the ages of six and fifteen, as long as the children attend a state school. Japanese schools are very disciplined, and teachers are highly respected. Exams are taken very seriously, and many children, from age six up to university entrance, go to private "crammers" for personal tutoring. This takes place outside normal school hours and can be quite costly.

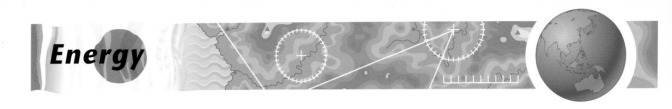

Energy

Japan's economy has a big weakness—it is short of energy resources. Japan has little oil and has used up its best coal.

The oil crises

Until 1973, Japan depended on cheap oil from the Middle East for industry, transportation, electricity generation, and heat for buildings. The **oil crises** in 1973 and 1979 forced Japan to rethink its energy policy.

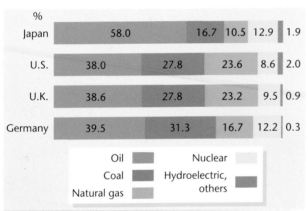

A International comparison of energy sources (1992)

Japan now uses oil more efficiently, and has reduced its dependence on oil from about 75 percent to about 50 percent. But three-quarters of Japan's oil still comes from the Middle East. Japan also uses more energy from other sources. Natural gas, which is **imported** mainly from Brunei and Indonesia, provides 10 percent of Japan's energy. Almost all of Japan's coal is imported from Australia and China.

Nuclear and hydroelectric power (HEP)

Japan has developed nuclear power to try to reduce oil imports. Japan has one of the biggest nuclear programs in the world, with 50 power stations operating or being built. They provide 10 percent of Japan's energy.

Japan has many mountains and lakes, but most of the rivers and drainage basins are too small to be of much use for **HEP**. Japan gets less than 2 percent of its energy from HEP.

B The distribution of nuclear power stations

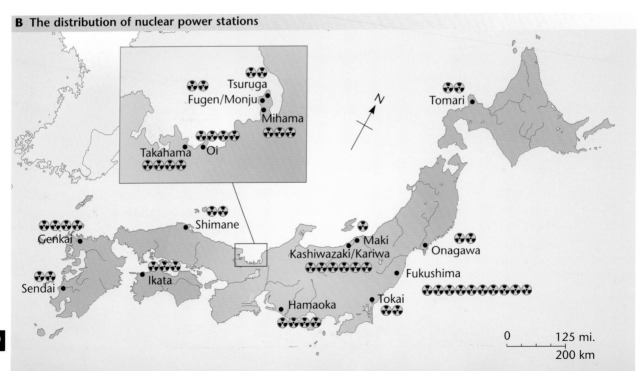

C This is the nuclear power station at Oi.

Alternatives

Today, 84 percent of Japan's energy comes from overseas. There are worries about nuclear power, so the Japanese are eager to find alternative sources of energy. They are studying wind, wave, solar, and **geothermal energy**. At the moment, however, none produces enough power at an economical price.

	1984	1994
In favor of more nuclear power stations	64%	67%
Should stop building nuclear power stations	14%	20%
Should stop generating nuclear power altogether	10%	7%
Don't know	12%	6%

D Public opinion about nuclear power

THE NUCLEAR DEBATE

The nuclear debate

The Oi Nuclear Power Station is one of a group of fifteen that has been built around Wakasa Bay on the Sea of Japan coast. This area has been chosen because it is a safe distance away from major centers of population. The sea provides power stations with large amounts of cooling water.

Safety is the main concern in the debate about nuclear power, although in Japan most people are in favor of developing nuclear power. There are three main problems:
* the risk of a major disaster, like the accident at Chernobyl, Russia in 1986, and at a plant processing fuel for use in the Joyo experimental fast-breeder reactor in Tokaimura, Japan, on September 30, 1999.
* the risk of smaller leaks of harmful radiation
* the problem of what to do with nuclear waste, which needs to be stored safely for thousands of years.

Nuclear power also has some advantages:
* It is a concentrated and powerful form of energy, so it needs less fuel and land.
* It produces small amounts of waste.
* It causes much less air pollution than burning coal, oil, or gas.

FACT FILE

Energy supply and consumption

	% of Japan's energy supply	
	1970	1995
Oil	72	56
Coal	20	17
Natural gas	1	10
Nuclear energy	0	14
Others	7	3

Energy consumption per person (lbs. per year)

Japan	8,501
Australia	11,775
France	8,911
Germany	9,101
U.K.	8,316
United States	17,238

Japan's energy consumption is remarkably low, given that it is one of the most successful economies in the world.

Leisure and Tourism

▶ **What do the Japanese do in their leisure time?**
▶ **Why is it important to the economy?**

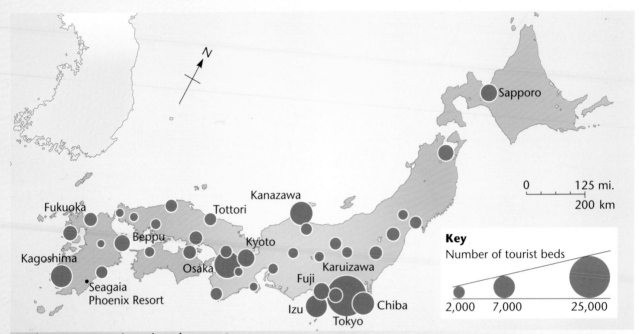

N

0   125 mi.
200 km

Sapporo

Kanazawa
Fukuoka   Tottori
Beppu   Kyoto
Kagoshima
Osaka   Karuizawa
Seagaia   Fuji
Phoenix Resort
Izu   Chiba
Tokyo

Key
Number of tourist beds

2,000   7,000   25,000

A These towns are Japan's major resorts.

Japanese people work hard, but leisure time is also more and more important. Traditional tourism is still popular, such as spending time at a hot spring resort like Karuizawa or playing *pachinko*—a type of pinball. But as people have more time and money to spend, the choice of things to do is widening. Near cities, theme parks, sports centers, and golf courses are being built. An example is Tokyo Disneyland, Japan's number one visitor attraction with seventeen million visitors in 1995. Unfortunately, these leisure facilities use up large amounts of farmland. On the coast, marinas are springing up, while ski runs are being carved out of mountainsides.

More leisure time and wealth allows more people to travel abroad; eleven million did so in 1995. In the opposite direction, three million foreign tourists visited Japan. The most popular destinations are Tokyo, Kyoto, Kanazawa, and Beppu.

KARUIZAWA: A HILL RESORT

Karuizawa is a famous resort in the volcanic hills of Honshu. Although it is 90 mi. (150 km) from Tokyo, good road and rail links mean thousands of people can take day trips there. It is famous for three attractions:
• its hot springs and traditional hotels
• its cool summer climate and forest walks
• its new winter sports facilities.

B Karuizawa is a popular destination.

THE SEAGAIA PHOENIX RESORT

This leisure complex is located on the coast of Miyazaki in southern Kyushu. It was opened in 1993, along with a golf course, tennis club, zoo, hotels, and a convention center. In its first full year of operation, it attracted nearly four million visitors. There is also a fine sandy beach there, but the main attraction is Ocean Dome. The Dome is the biggest indoor water park in the world and can hold up to 10,000 visitors. It is 985 ft. (300 m) long, 330 ft. (100 m) wide, and 125 ft. (38 m) high. It has a sliding roof, and waves as high as 8 ft. (2.5 m) can be created.

Developments like this have benefits and costs. They create jobs in rural areas, well away from the major cities. But they also impact the environment. Habitats and wildlife are disturbed, while large buildings spoil the coastal scenery.

C The Ocean Dome water park attracts many tourists.

	1965	1975	1985	1995
Japanese leaving	373	2,489	4,024	11,291
Foreigners entering	160	821	1,832	2,855

D Departure and entry of tourists (1,000s)

Top ten overseas destinations of Japanese tourists (1,000s)			
United States	3,067	Taiwan	489
South Korea	1,234	China	441
Hong Kong	738	Thailand	313
Australia	594	U.K.	256
Singapore	553	France	249

Top ten overseas tourists visiting Japan (1,000s)			
Taiwan	567	Thailand	31
South Korea	397	Brazil	25
United States	214	Hong Kong	23
U.K.	120	Australia	23
Canada	40	Germany	21

E Overseas tourism

More leisure time is important for the economy, as people spend more money on tourism in Japan and overseas. This money comes from what people have earned from their jobs in **primary**, **secondary**, and **tertiary** activities. It helps create more tertiary jobs, especially in rural and remote areas. This can help reduce rural **migration** to the cities.

FACT FILE

Leisure activities and spending
The table shows the ten most popular leisure activities in Japan in rank order.

1 Dining out
2 Visiting a hot spring
3 Driving
4 Karaoke
5 Drinking in a bar or pub
6 Visiting a zoo, botanical garden, etc.
7 Watching videos
8 Listening to music
9 Visiting an amusement park
10 Lottery

As leisure becomes a more important part of everyday life in Japan, the amount of money being spent on leisure activities is rising. The proportion of household income now spent on leisure is eight percent. That is more than is spent on medical care. Increased spending on leisure is helping to create still more tertiary sector jobs, and more facilities are being built. For example, the number of restaurants in Japan has increased by 60 percent since 1970, and golf practice ranges and golf courses have more than doubled.

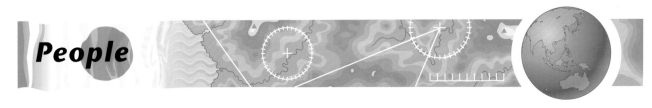

People

> ▶ **How have Japanese people made their country so successful?**

Japanese people have a strong national identity and culture. They have their own values, attitudes, and codes of behavior, in spite of the "westernization" of Japan since 1945. Some characteristics of the Japanese people have been particularly important when it comes to explaining the country's economic success. They have helped make Japan a world superstar and have made up for the country's shortage of natural resources.

A The Japanese labor force is hardworking.

Qualities at work

First, as a rule, Japanese people try hard not to be different from each other. What many want most of all is to be accepted and respected as members of a group. That group may be linked to work, leisure, or the home. Belonging to a group gives people a sense of security and well-being—known as *amae*. Being able to work in groups is good for the workplace, as well as for society.

Second, most Japanese people believe that working hard is a virtue. Everyone is expected to do his or her best, regardless of job or status.

Also, working hours are longer and leisure time shorter than in many other countries.

There is a tradition that Japanese companies care for their employees. Once a firm has taken workers on, they have jobs for life. Firms can provide housing and medical care and may arrange marriages or vacations. In return, workers stay loyal and committed to the firm.

Running a business is rather different in Japan. Many firms reach agreement by involving workers in decisions. There is not a "them and us" feeling between workers and their bosses. They are part of the same "team." So strikes are uncommon, and there is little need for strong trade unions. Although the rate of unemployment has risen, it is well below that of most European countries.

Face

As a people, the Japanese are honest, polite, and law-abiding. Part of the reason is that keeping the respect of other people is very important to them. As one Japanese person wrote: "We are anxious what others think of us, and what we fear most is loss of **face**." Keeping face has also helped the economy, because workers have been prepared to work hard for the sake of Japan.

	Average monthly working hours	Membership of trade union (% of workforce)	Unemployment (% of workforce)
1970	186.6	35.4	0.9
1975	172.0	34.4	1.5
1980	175.7	30.8	1.6
1985	175.8	28.9	2.1
1990	171.0	25.2	3.0

B Some trends at work

WOMEN IN THE WORKFORCE

Sayuri Nakamura is one of Japan's increasing number of working women. There are now over two million of them, but they are still only 3 percent of the workforce, compared with more than 60 percent in the U.S. Sayuri graduated from college fourteen years ago; since then, she has worked for a large computer software company. In that time, she has married and had two daughters, but has continued to work.

Sayuri's husband has a job in a publishing company. But because of the cost of housing in Tokyo and of raising a family, they need both incomes. Sayuri has been able to continue her career because her company has a nursery for employees' children. Sayuri's mother lives close by, so she can help with child care.

Nearly three-quarters of Japan's working women are married. Although Japanese society still expects women to quit their jobs when they start families, more and more are taking part-time work or continuing their careers. So Sayuri is among the first of a new generation in Japan.

C The Nakamura family is typical of Japanese families today.

FACT FILE

Religion
The main religions in Japan are Shintoism and Buddhism. All but a small percentage of the population follow Shintoism, and most of them are also Buddhists. This is possible because Shintoism is polytheistic; people who follow Shintoism believe in many gods, and there is nothing in it to keep people from following another religion as well.

Shintoism is the older religion of the two, and grew out of the everyday life of Japanese people in early times. It has a lot to do with fertility, death, the natural world, and the seasons. Shinto gods—and there are thousands of them—are worshiped at shrines. People go to a shrine when a child is born or when someone marries. Prayers are said at shrines for various things, including success at work, help in passing exams, or protection from accidents. But Shintoism has no leaders, such as priests; there are no holy writings, such as the Bible; and communal worship—in the form of a service—is rare.

The Japanese have a strong belief in the continuity of life and family ancestors, which is central to Buddhism. The many temples found all over Japan are Buddhist.

The Japanese constitution guarantees religious freedom, so there is no state religion, and religious education is forbidden in schools.

Population Change

▶ **Why has Japan's population structure changed?**
▶ **What effects will this have?**

The population of Japan is now about 126 million. People live at an average density of 865 people per square mi. (332 per square km). But since only a quarter of Japan's land is suitable for settlement, its settled areas probably show average densities of more than 2,600 people per square mi. (1,000 per square km)—some of the world's highest.

During the twentieth century, the population of Japan has increased by nearly three times, from 44 to 126 million. The **demographic transition** model (graph **A**) helps explain this population growth. In the past 100 years, Japan has moved from Stage 2 to Stage 4.

Why has the population grown so much?

You can find the answer to this question by investigating **birth rates** and **death rates** using graph **A**. The birth rate today is 10 births per 1,000 people, or less than one-third of what it was in 1900. The reasons for this fall include
- more birth control
- the high cost of housing
- a more material outlook on life
- a change in attitudes about marriage and family life
- more women preferring careers to raising children.

As the birth rate has dropped, the average family size has fallen to 3.25 people. Only half of Japanese households today contain one or more children.

To explain why Japan's population has increased, we also need to look at changes in the death rate. This has fallen too, from 24 to 8 deaths per 1,000 people. The reasons for this include
- better diet
- improved housing
- healthier environment
- better medical care.

Falling death rates have meant an increase in people's **life expectancy**, especially since 1945. For men, it has risen from 65 to 77 years, and for women, from 70 to 83 years.

An aging population

The difference between the birth rate and death rate is called the rate of **natural increase**. In Japan today, it is 2 per 1,000 people. Although the natural increase rate is a lot lower than in the past, the number of people continues to grow because the total population is much larger.

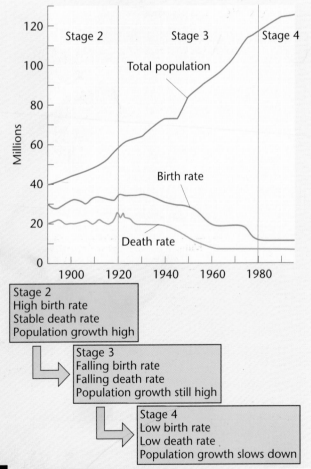

Stage 2
High birth rate
Stable death rate
Population growth high

Stage 3
Falling birth rate
Falling death rate
Population growth still high

Stage 4
Low birth rate
Low death rate
Population growth slows down

A The demographic transition model

The age-sex pyramid shows the balance between males and females and the balance among different age groups. The pyramids show that the Japanese population is gradually getting older; this is sometimes called the "silvering" of the people.

D Japan's population is aging.

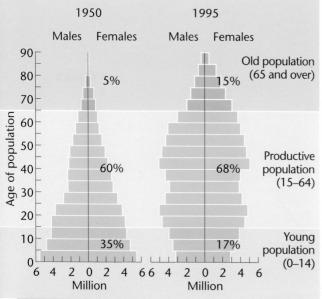

B Japan's changing age–sex pyramid (1950–1995)

It means that there are more old people who depend on the working population to provide for them, while at the same time the percentage of children is decreasing. These changes will have important consequences for Japanese society in the future.

Age	5	10	15	20	25	30	35	40	45	50	55	60	65	70	75	80	85	90
Male (millions)	3.0	3.1	3.5	3.6	3.7	3.5	3.2	3.4	3.7	4.0	5.0	3.7	3.5	3.6	3.6	2.0	1.0	0.5
Female (millions)	2.7	2.8	3.1	3.4	3.4	3.0	2.9	3.0	3.4	4.0	4.7	4.0	3.8	4.0	4.2	3.2	2.0	1.5

C Estimated figures for population in 2025

FACT FILE

Causes of death

At 8 deaths per 1,000 people, Japan has one of the lowest death rates in the world. Better medical care has helped to lower that rate. Since 1981, cancer has been the leading cause of death. The death rate by cancer has risen from 77 per 100,000 population in 1950 to 182 in 1991. Heart disease is the second leading cause of death and is also on the rise. Some think that this is partly due to the change in the Japanese diet, and in particular to the eating of more meat and dairy products. Lung disorders have declined a great deal as killers. This may be due to the reduction of atmospheric pollution.

	Male deaths (1991)	Female deaths (1991)
Cancer	143,475	89,252
Heart disease	83,646	85,232
Brain disease	55,740	62,708
Pneumonia and bronchitis	43,372	32,979
Accidents	22,879	10,276
Suicide	12,477	7,398
Liver disease	11,438	5,476
Tuberculosis	2,449	876

A Nation of City Dwellers

▶ **Why do people live in cities?**
▶ **What are the results of city growth?**

Urbanization

Today, around 80 percent of Japanese people live in urban areas. Throughout this century, Japanese towns and cities have grown rapidly, a process known as **urbanization**. Until recently, the more towns and cities have grown, the more they have attracted industry, services, and even more people.

Rural–urban migration

The populations of towns and cities grow in two ways—by **natural increase**, when more people are born than die, and by rural–urban **migration**, when people move in from the countryside. These migrants from rural areas are often young people who may also have children once they have settled in the city. Throughout most of the last 100 years, Japan has experienced massive rural–urban migration. The countryside has been drained of people as cities have mushroomed. Graph **B** shows the speed at which Japan has changed from a rural to an urban society.

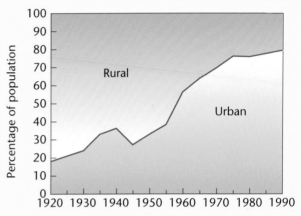

B The urbanization of Japan

The distribution of cities

Japan has eleven cities with more than one million people. All except one, Sapporo, are located in the Pacific Belt. At the eastern end of the Pacific Belt, four major cities—Tokyo, Yokohama, Kawasaki, and Chiba—are so close that they have grown together into one huge metropolitan area. This wraps around the shores of Tokyo Bay and contains a total population of around 25 million. Two other metropolitan areas have formed, from the cities of Osaka, Kyoto, and Kobe, and from the area around Nagoya. In turn, the three metropolitan areas are growing together to form a mammoth, elongated urban area called a **megalopolis**, stretching from Tokyo to Kobe. Outside Tokaido megalopolis, growth around five other cities—Sapporo, Sendai, Hiroshima, and a combined Kitakyushu and Fukuoka—is creating four new metropolitan areas.

Decentralization

Since the 1970s, the rate of urbanization in Japan has slowed. People and some businesses are now moving out of congested central areas to city suburbs. Some are even moving out of the metropolitan areas to rings of growing **commuter** towns. Reasons for this **decentralization** include

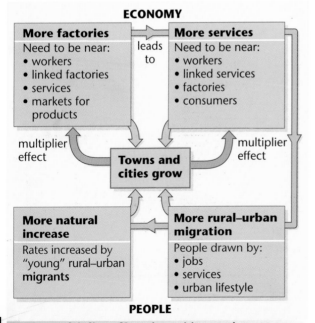

A The **multiplier effect**: how cities continue to grow

- high costs of city land and buildings
- congestion
- poor quality city environments
- better public transportation and communications
- changes in people's tastes.

Today, decentralization mainly affects larger cities and occurs over relatively short distances. The concentration of urban growth in the heart of the Pacific Belt looks set to continue in the twenty-first century.

Tokyo	8.2	Fukuoka	1.3
Yokohama	3.3	Kawasaki	1.2
Osaka	2.6	Hiroshima	1.1
Nagoya	2.2	Kitakyushu	1.0
Sapporo	1.8	Sendai	1.0
Kobe	1.5	Chiba	0.9
Kyoto	1.5		

C The major cities of Japan (populations in millions)

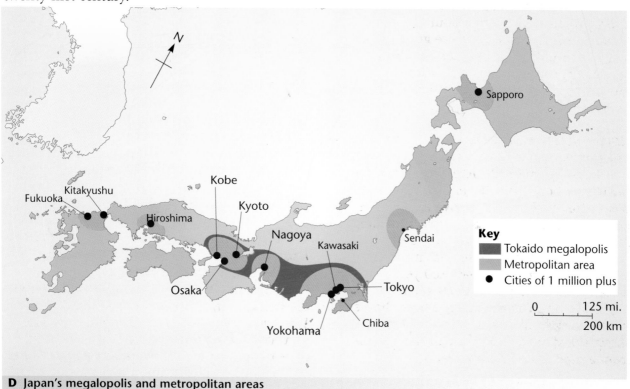

D Japan's megalopolis and metropolitan areas

Key
- Tokaido megalopolis
- Metropolitan area
- Cities of 1 million plus

0 — 125 mi. / 200 km

FACT FILE

Crime

Crime rates in Japan are noticeably lower than in most other developed countries. Tokyo is said to be the safest of the world's major cities. One of the main reasons is that the possession of guns and swords is severely restricted. Another is the Japanese concern about **face**: to be exposed as a criminal would be a serious loss of face. Organized crime—run by gangsters known as the *yakuza*—mainly involves prostitution and pornography, fraud and fixing, and loans and debt collection.

Juvenile delinquency has decreased since 1983, when it was at its highest. Violence in schools and in the home, which at one time filled the newspapers in Japan, is falling. So, too, is the number of youths arrested for drug offenses.

	Crimes per 100,000 population		Arrest rate (%)	
	Murder	Theft	Murder	Theft
Japan	1.0	1,226	96.0	30.7
U.K.	2.5	8,135	94.2	22.0
Germany	4.1	4,906	90.7	26.9
France	4.7	3,607	73.9	12.4
U.S.	9.3	4,903	64.6	17.7

Tokaido Megalopolis

▶ **Why is the Pacific Belt continuing to grow?**
▶ **What is it like to live in Tokaido megalopolis?**

A This satellite image shows Hiroshima, which is likely to become part of Tokaido megalopolis.

Benefits and costs

The urban areas of the Pacific Belt continue to grow, attracting industry, business, and people. City suburbs fill in the rural spaces between towns and cities, helped by efficient transportation links. In these ways, that part of the Pacific Belt between Tokyo and Kobe has become linked into a single urban system, called Tokaido **megalopolis**. This growing area contains nearly two-thirds of all Japan's population and manufacturing. Most of Japan's specialized services are also found here. If

urbanization continues, Tokaido megalopolis will eventually extend further westward to engulf Hiroshima and reach as far as Kitakyushu and Fukuoka in northern Kyushu. It will stretch the length of the Pacific Belt. The fast and efficient transportation links needed to extend the megalopolis in this way already exist.

Why does Tokaido megalopolis continue to grow?

The answer lies in the enormous population and wealth of the Pacific Belt. Industries and services need access to plenty of people, both as workers and customers. In turn, as cities prosper and grow, more industries and services grow to meet the needs of these people and their families. Other industries and services are attracted by linkages between businesses, so the region grows still more. An unstoppable upward spiral of growth is created.

Living in Tokaido megalopolis

What is the quality of life like for people living in Tokaido megalopolis? Let us try to answer this question by looking at three different aspects. Next to food, housing is probably the most important. Table **B** compares the housing situation in Tokyo, at the eastern end of Tokaido megalopolis, with that in three other major world cities.

Crime statistics show that Japanese people are law-abiding. The murder rate in Japan is very low, and mugging is virtually unknown, so people are very safe on the streets of Tokaido megalopolis.

	Tokyo	London	Paris	New York
Average price of residential land (¥1,000 per square ft.)	52.0	2.8	2.7	0.9
Average house price (¥1,000)	132	62	36	33
Area of park per resident (square ft.)	29.1	247.6	124.9	275.6

B Comparison of housing in four major cities (¥ = yen—Japanese currency)

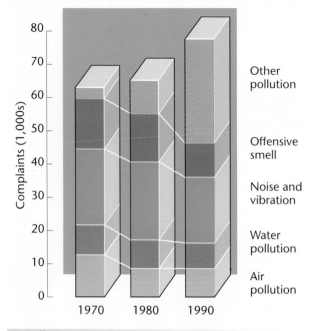

C Pollution complaints

Reducing environmental pollution is only one planning objective in Tokaido megalopolis. Others include:
- improving transportation and reducing traffic congestion
- opening up the central areas by lowering land-use densities
- encouraging businesses to move to the suburbs (**decentralization**)
- improving the quality of housing and services.

Achieving these objectives is made difficult by one basic feature of Tokaido megalopolis—the shortage and high cost of land.

D Thousands live close together in congested housing.

Since the bad days of the 1960s, much has been done to reduce pollution levels in Tokaido megalopolis. Rivers and coastal waters are now much cleaner, but other forms of pollution, like smell, noise, and vibration, are still problems. Visual pollution is another feature of the Tokaido megalopolis environment. Garish advertising and skylines cluttered by pylons and overhead cables disfigure the built environment. Although these forms of pollution may be less damaging to human health than air and water pollution, they do affect people's safety and quality of life. Congestion, pace, and stress are part of everyday life in Tokaido megalopolis. Finding ways of disposing of increasing amounts of garbage remains a serious problem.

FACT FILE

The cost of land for housing

A shortage of usable space is one of the major problems of modern Japan. As with any other resource, its price goes up when it is in short supply. The rise in price has been greatest in the six largest cities. Between 1955 and 1990, the average price of land being sold for housing increased nearly 2,000 times. Since then, however, the price has begun to fall. The government decided to get tough with people speculating in land. As a result, the price of residential land has already fallen by as much as one-third. That is particularly good for people looking for new homes in the suburbs of the largest cities. It not only means cheaper houses, but it may also mean a small increase in the average dwelling size.

5 REGIONAL DIFFERENCES

Around the Regions

▶ **What are the differences between the regions? What are the similarities?**

Region	% share total area	% mountains	% lowland	Population (millions)	% share total pop.	%share GDP	% share primary sector output	% share secondary sector output	% share tertiary sector output
Hokkaido	22.1	49.0	11.7	5.7	4.5	3.8	10.9	2.6	4.1
Tohoku	17.7	62.0	14.3	9.8	7.8	6.3	16.2	5.3	6.3
Kanto	8.6	40.4	20.7	39.5	31.5	36.6	16.5	35.7	38.3
Chubu	17.6	70.9	14.9	21.4	17.0	17.4	15.9	21.4	15.1
Kinki	8.8	64.1	16.9	22.5	17.9	18.2	8.2	19.5	17.9
Chugoku	8.4	74.1	9.6	7.8	6.2	5.9	6.4	6.2	5.7
Shikoku	5.0	79.9	10.1	4.2	3.4	2.6	6.4	2.3	2.7
Kyushu	11.8	62.7	12.3	14.7	11.7	9.2	19.5	7.0	9.9

B Comparing statistics in the different regions

For the purposes of government, Japan is divided into 47 **prefectures.** They are the equivalents of American states and are grouped into eight regions, called *chiho.*

Hokkaido
Hokkaido is the most northern island. Its harsh environment and distance from the Pacific Belt make it the most sparsely populated area of Japan. Hokkaido's economy is based on **primary sector** activities, especially farming. Tourism is becoming more important.

A Regions of Japan

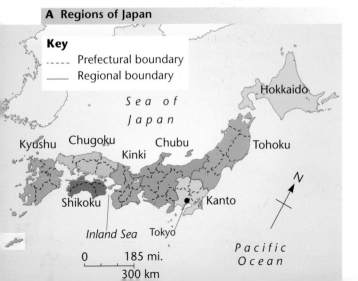

Tohoku
This is one of five regions on Honshu, the main island. It is another thinly populated area, cut off by mountains. **Bullet trains** and an expressway have made it more **accessible.** This is Japan's main rice-growing region. Sendai, a growing city, is a new center for industry and offices.

Kanto
This region is truly the heart of Japan. It contains Japan's biggest concentration of population. Tokyo, the capital city, is a center of manufacturing and services. Yokohama is Japan's leading port, and Kawasaki is a major center of heavy industry. The Kanto Plain is important for farming geared to the needs of the huge urban market.

Chubu
This region cuts a section across central Honshu, so it has three different parts. Along the Pacific Coast, Nagoya is the main city. It is a major center of the car industry. Inland, large parts of the mountainous area are protected as national parks, producing much of Japan's **hydroelectric power.** On the Sea of Japan coast, industry and rice growing are important.

C Hokkaido has many farms but few people.

Kinki

This is a lowland region containing three major cities: Kyoto, Osaka, and Kobe. It is Japan's second most important industrial region.

Chugoku

This small region is in the "toe" of Honshu. Inland, it is mountainous, and the Sea of Japan coast is remote and undeveloped. But the Inland Sea coast has good transportation links and is growing fast. Hiroshima is the main city.

Shikoku

This is the smallest of the main islands. New bridges over the Inland Sea connect Shikoku to Honshu. These will encourage development along the north coast. However, the rest of the island is mountainous and remote.

Kyushu

Kyushu has good transportation links with Honshu. Its northern and southern areas are very different. Two-thirds of the population live in the north of the island, an old industrial area centered in Kitakyushu and Fukuoka. The south is mainly a farming area, but it is also attracting **high-tech** industry. The south's subtropical climate and volcanic scenery attract tourists.

Japan's regions show similarities and differences. All of them have a mixture of lowland and upland. In all of them, the lowlands and coast have attracted settlement and development. However, differences in climate mean differences in farming and living conditions.

D Kyushu is a center for many industries.

FACT FILE

Prefectures

Japan is divided into 47 prefectures. These are smaller areas within each region. They are not closely tied to the Japanese government, so they have considerable freedom in matters such as taxation, lawmaking, and taking initiatives. Individual prefectures can make more decisions for themselves, about such things as building a new port or setting up a new university. This freedom of action can be very important for economic growth. The success of individual prefectures' economies is greatly affected by the drive and enterprise of prefectural governments. Prefectural enterprise can often make up for a poor location and a lack of resources.

Because prefectural government is so important, the capitals of the prefectures have become significant cities. The various government departments are concentrated there. These prominent cities attract private and **public services**, as well as many other businesses, and they rank above any other cities within each prefecture.

Core and Periphery

▶ **Why does a core region develop?**

▶ **How does the core affect the periphery?**

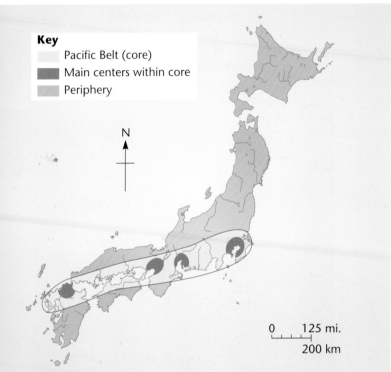

Key

- Pacific Belt (core)
- Main centers within core
- Periphery

N

0 — 125 mi.
200 km

A Japan's core and periphery

B Net migration

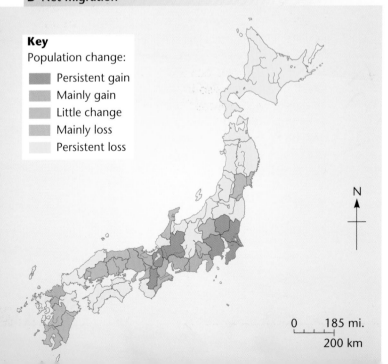

Key

Population change:

- Persistent gain
- Mainly gain
- Little change
- Mainly loss
- Persistent loss

N

0 — 185 mi.
200 km

Winners and losers

As we have seen, some parts of Japan are wealthier than others. Together, Kanto, Chubu, and Kinki have over 70 percent of Japan's economic wealth. The other regions produce the rest, but they make up 65 percent of the land area. There are economic winners and losers, as in other countries, like the United States.

The core

Economic growth in Japan is concentrated in the Pacific Belt, the wealthiest part of the country. This is Japan's economic heart, or **core**. In fact, Japan's core region is shaped like a sausage, stretching from Tokyo around to northern Kyushu. Even the core has its own fastest growing areas, especially around Tokyo.

Advantages and disadvantages of the core

Japan's core first developed around the Inland Sea, which was the best region for settlement, farming, fishing, and shipping. This initial advantage was enough for the region to get ahead of other parts of Japan. Once the core began to grow, it began to attract more people and economic activities like a magnet. There were many benefits in locating there:

- Being close to other businesses cut down transportation costs.
- Businesses could sell their products to the growing, wealthy population.
- The region attracted skilled workers.

The core spread eastward along the lowlands of the Pacific coast.

There are also costs for businesses and people in the core:

- Competition for space means high land prices.
- Competition for skilled workers leads to higher wages and labor costs.
- Lack of space leads to congestion, cramped housing, and a poor environment.
- Pressure on the environment leads to pollution of air and water.

All this encourages land **reclamation**, which takes its own toll on the environment.

The periphery

The poorer regions outside the core are known as the **periphery.** The main problem for Japan is that as the core grows, it sucks in people and resources from the regions in the periphery, so they lose out while the core gains. It is this loss of population that hurts regions in the periphery most. It is usually the younger and more able people who leave. They are attracted to the core by better prospects, like better jobs, higher wages, and more services. But when these people go, they can leave things worse for those who are left.

Hope for the periphery

There is some hope for the periphery. People in the booming core region need things that the periphery can supply. People in urban areas need food; this could give Japanese farmers in the periphery the chance to modernize. The countryside of the periphery offers a chance for busy people from the core to escape for leisure and recreation. The core regions also use up huge amounts of energy, while the periphery has empty spaces for nuclear power stations and lakes and rivers for **hydroelectric power.**

LAND RECLAMATION

Because of the shortage of space, the Japanese have had to create land themselves, especially by reclaiming land from the sea. In Tokyo Bay, over 247,000 acres (100,000 hectares) of new land have been reclaimed. The size of the bay has been reduced by pushing out the shoreline and by creating huge artificial islands in the bay (map **C**). The new land has been used to extend the port and Haneda airport, as well as for industry, new offices, and housing and leisure complexes. The costs are enormous, but developers are willing to pay the price, especially around Tokyo and other big cities where the demand for space is highest.

Key
- Reclaimed land
- Old coastline
- Built–up area not on reclaimed land

C This land was reclaimed from Tokyo Bay.

FACT FILE

Social class

Although Japan can be divided into core and periphery—prosperous and not-so-prosperous areas—Japanese society is relatively classless. Today, the people with high social status are mainly

- executives in major business companies
- high-level government officials
- professors in the top universities
- professional people, like surgeons, lawyers, etc.
- members of the Japanese parliament.

Many people in such positions today started from modest beginnings. In Japan, a person's social origin has little to do with his or her chances of reaching a high social status. Individual effort and achievement in education are the two key factors. There is, however, one underprivileged group known as the *burakumin* or *eta*. Historically, this class of outcasts was made up of people earning their living by slaughtering livestock and working leather. Today, the class also includes prostitutes, beggars, and tramps.

Transportation and Accessibility

Good transportation links are very important in Japan. Good **accessibility** is needed because

- Japan is a nation of islands that need to be linked;
- three-quarters of the country is mountainous;
- population and industry are located on separate small lowlands around the coast.

Rail network (*shinkansen* lines)

Road network (expressways)

A Most major transportation networks

Rail transportation

Japan is famous for its high-speed passenger **bullet trains**, or *shinkansen*. There are three lines out of Tokyo: to Fukuoka, Morioka, and Niigata. These are being extended and made even faster. In towns and cities, subways and suburban trains play an important part in getting **commuters** to work.

LINKING THE ISLANDS

Before 1942, the four main islands were linked only by ferry services. Since then, with help from the government, a number of bridges and tunnels have been built to join the islands. Some of these are spectacular feats of engineering.

The first direct links by tunnel and suspension bridge were built between Honshu and Kyushu. Hokkaido and Honshu are now connected by the Seikan rail tunnel, the longest underwater tunnel in the world.

The Inland Sea is being crossed by three bridge links from Shikoku to Honshu. The bridges use small islands as stepping stones. All of them have two tiers, one for road and one for rail. The bridge across the Akashi Straits to Kobe will be the longest in the world. However, the recent Kobe earthquake moved the bridge over 3 feet (1 meter) to the west.

B This is one of Shikoku's new bridges.

Road transportation

There are now more than 60 million vehicles on Japan's roads, 39 million of them cars. In cities, many people use cars for commuting, in spite of the availability of public transportation. Car use is increasing, and traffic congestion is often severe. Outside the cities, Japan's mountains and islands make building roads difficult. There is really only one national expressway, from Aomori in northern Honshu to Kagoshima in southern Kyushu.

Air transportation

Air transportation within Japan is not important compared with road and rail. It is used mainly to move people, as well as some high-value goods

	1970	1980	1993
Passengers (% of total)			
Rail	40.4	34.8	27.6
Road	29.1	19.1	10.0
Car	30.1	45.8	62.1
Air	0.0	0.0	0.1
Ship	0.4	0.3	0.2
Freight (% of total)			
Rail	4.8	2.7	1.3
Road	88.0	88.9	90.5
Ship	7.2	8.4	8.2

C Domestic transportation (1970–93)

KANSAI INTERNATIONAL AIRPORT

This airport in Osaka Bay opened in 1994. It was built 3 mi. (5 km) from the coast on land **reclaimed** from the sea. Although Kansai airport is on an artificial island, it still has very good transportation links. A jet foil service runs from Kobe, and there is a bridge to the mainland for express road and rail services. Aviation fuel is brought in by tanker to a special pier.

D This is an aerial view of Kansai airport.

like microchips and flowers. By contrast, international air travel is booming. The volume of traffic is so great that Tokyo has two international airports, with four others in other parts of Japan.

Summing up

Japan has invested huge amounts of money in improving transportation links. Modern transportation is needed to link the lowlands, and to link the more remote **periphery** with the **core** region. The hope is that better accessibility will encourage economic growth in the periphery. However, traffic congestion is a serious problem in many parts of the core.

FACT FILE

Commuting

Most Japanese cities have strong central areas, in which jobs and services are highly concentrated. This concentration, in turn, leads to huge daily movements of people from their homes in the suburbs and outlying settlements into central city areas. In Tokyo, the daily volume of passengers traveling into the central area is more than two million. A great strain is put on city transportation networks, and severe traffic jams are part of everyday city life. The largest cities look to the railways to help solve the problem. Subway systems have the advantage of not using much surface space, but they are very expensive to build.

Japan's major subway (underground) systems (1994)

	Operating distance		Number of lines	Passengers carried daily (thousands)
	mi.	km		
Tokyo	143	230	12	9,037
Osaka	66	106	7	2,667
Nagoya	48	77	6	1,402
Sapporo	25	40	3	748

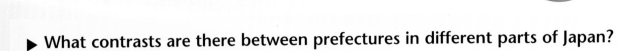

Three Prefectures

▶ **What contrasts are there between prefectures in different parts of Japan?**

This section looks at three **prefectures** located in different parts of Japan. The three show inequalities in wealth and in their future prospects. One is part of Japan's **core**; the other two are in the **periphery**.

These three prefectures show basic differences in geography and development. The difference in development is largely the result of differences in distance from the core.

	Chiba	Miyagi	Kochi
Total area (square mi.)	1,962	2,649	2,743
Mountains (%)	8	31	86
Urban area (%)	29	7	5
Population (1990)	5,550,000	2,249,000	825,000
Population change (1980–90)	+79,100	+33,000	–17,500
Manufacturing (% total employed)	21	17	12
Services (% total employed)	71	68	67
GDP (billion yen)	16	7	2

A Comparative statistics for three prefectures

CHIBA PREFECTURE

Chiba prefecture

Chiba is on the eastern side of Tokyo Bay. It forms the eastern limit of Japan's core, the Pacific Belt. Recent suburban growth along railway lines and main roads has joined it to the Tokyo metropolitan area and to Tokaido **megalopolis**.

Many of the working people **commute** into Tokyo. On land **reclaimed** from the bay, there is a fringe of waterfront industries, such as oil refining, petrochemicals, and iron and steel. There is also housing on this land. Port facilities have been built to allow the **import** of oil and raw materials and the **export** of manufactured goods. Narita Airport is Japan's leading international airport. It was built in the 1970s amid much public protest. Local people were angry about the destruction of over 1,000 homes, the loss of farmland, and the great increase in noise.

The prospects for this prosperous prefecture are good. But there are challenges, such as making sure that future growth does not cause congestion or too much damage to the environment.

B The Tokyo Bay waterfront is home to many leading Japanese industrie

C Location of the three prefectures

KOCHI PREFECTURE

This prefecture in southern Shikoku is made up of a long coastal plain surrounded by mountains. Although there are now bridges linking Shikoku to Honshu, this part of the island remains cut off from the rest of the country. Things are beginning to change slowly. Instead of growing two crops of rice each year, farmers are now exploiting the warm climate by producing early vegetables, fruit, and flowers for the major urban markets of the Pacific Belt. Improvement of the Kochi airport would help, and would also attract more tourists to this quiet and unspoiled corner of the country. But will it do anything to halt the loss of population from the prefecture? One problem is that the Kochi coast is the part of Japan most exposed to **typhoons** sweeping in from the Pacific.

MIYAGI PREFECTURE

This is one of the few prefectures in the Japanese periphery now enjoying economic growth and rising prosperity. It is part of Japan's main rice-producing region. Improvement of transportation has been the key factor in turning around Miyagi's fortunes. Travel times over the 185 mi. (300 km) or so from Tokyo have been reduced to a few hours. A new port has been built at Shiogama. This improved **accessibility** has encouraged the setting up of new industries and offices in and around the city of Sendai. If Miyagi continues to grow, it could become part of Japan's core. In the meantime, the challenge is to try to spread future growth more evenly across the prefecture.

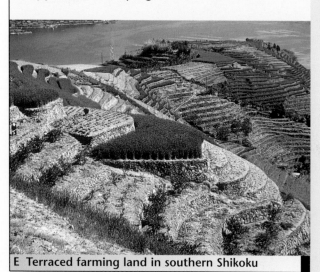

E Terraced farming land in southern Shikoku

D Sendai is becoming a dynamic center in Miyagi in the Japanese periphery.

FACT FILE

Economic indicators (1990)

	Chiba	Miyagi	Kochi
Rice production (1,000 tons)	343	484	74
Working forest (1,000 acres)	2.2	7.7	9.9
Fish catches (1,000 tons)	372	593	149
Iron and steel output (billion yen)	1,629	133	24
Electrical goods (billion yen)	1,142	812	16
Processed food (billion yen)	980	613	65
Retail sales (billion yen)	4,474	1,166	731
Motor vehicles owned (1,000)	2,326	1,088	434
Housing land (1,000 yen per square ft.)	24.9	5.7	4.3
Primary school teachers	18,477	8,445	4,060
Hospital beds (1,000)	50.4	25.3	21.8
Local taxes (billion yen)	689,652	237,907	67,917

6 ► JAPAN AND THE GLOBAL COMMUNITY

Trade

► **Why is international trade so important to Japan?**
► **How have Japan's exports and imports changed?**

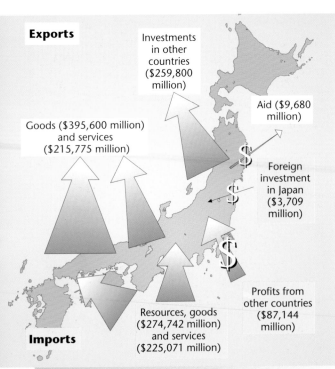

A Japan's international economy

Japan's international economy

Japan's economy today is truly global. There are few parts of the world that do not have some contact with Japan. Developing an international economy has helped make it one of the wealthiest countries in the world. Through the three links of trade, investment, and aid, Japan is able to

- obtain resources
- reach foreign markets
- make profits
- gain economic influence in other parts of the world.

Through these links, the economy draws more of its energy and strength from abroad.

Overseas trade is selling and buying with other countries. It works in two directions. For example, Japan makes cars and sells them abroad. These are **exports**. To make more cars, raw materials and energy are needed, so the money earned is used to buy these from other countries. These are **imports**.

Exports

Exports are goods or services that Japan sells to other countries. The Japanese economy is so strong that it creates around 10 percent of all world exports. Exports have changed much since 1955. The biggest growth has been in machinery and equipment. This includes the consumer goods for which Japan is world famous, such as cars and electronic goods.

Exports	1955	1965	1975	1985	1995
Machinery and equipment	12.4	42.1	61.3	71.8	76.0
Metals	19.2	13.9	17.8	10.5	6.1
Chemicals	5.1	6.5	5.9	4.4	6.0
Textile products	37.3	16.3	5.1	3.6	2.1
Other manufactures	19.7	17.6	8.9	8.9	9.3
Foodstuffs	6.3	3.6	1.0	0.8	0.5
Imports					
Foodstuffs	25.3	18.0	15.2	12.0	17.0
Raw materials	27.4	39.4	20.2	13.9	10.4
Mineral fuels	11.7	19.9	44.3	43.1	17.4
Manufactured goods	13.1	22.7	20.3	43.2	55.2

B The changing make-up of exports and imports (%)

Imports

Imports are goods that Japan buys from other countries. They are mainly things Japan cannot produce itself, like oil and other raw materials. Changes in industry mean that Japan imports less fuel and raw materials than in the past.

The balance of trade

Japan's success in selling its goods overseas is shown in the **balance of trade**—the difference between exports and imports. Japan's exports are valued at $120 billion more than its imports, which is a huge trade surplus. With some of Japan's trading partners, the surplus is so large that it causes ill feeling, known as **trade friction**. Some trading partners threaten to protect themselves by making it more difficult for Japan to export to them.

Japan also trades in services, such as global transportation and travel, investment, research, and development. Here, Japan imports more services than it exports, and so has a small trade deficit of $10 billion. However, overall Japan has a favorable balance of payments.

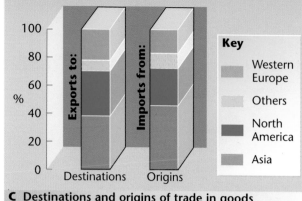

C Destinations and origins of trade in goods

	Exports %	Imports%
Hong Kong	6.5	0.8
South Korea	6.2	4.9
Taiwan	6.0	3.9
Singapore	5.0	1.7
China	4.5	10.0
Thailand	3.7	3.0
Malaysia	3.1	3.0
Indonesia	1.9	4.7
Philippines	1.5	1.0
India	0.5	1.0
Vietnam	0.1	0.5
Others	0.8	10.6
ASIA	39.8	45.1

D Japan's exports and imports for Asia (1994)

FACT FILE

The value of the yen

One of the clearest measures of Japan's economic success has been the increase in the value of its currency, the yen. The table shows how much the yen has appreciated, or increased in value, against the United States dollar. Today, the Japanese yen challenges the U.S. dollar as the world's most important currency.

The increasing value of the yen has been a mixed blessing for Japan. On the one hand, a strong yen buys more. This helps imports. On the other hand, a strong yen makes exporting more difficult, because more foreign currency is needed to buy Japanese goods. Japanese goods become more expensive.

Year	U.S. dollar exchange rate (yen)
1960	362
1965	361
1970	358
1975	297
1980	227
1985	239
1990	145
1995	94

Overseas Investment and Aid

▶ How and why does Japan invest abroad?

In addition to its world trade, Japan's economy is becoming more international through overseas investment and **foreign aid**. Overseas investment can happen in three ways:

- setting up **branch plants** in other countries
- arranging **joint ventures** to share technology and ideas
- putting money into overseas companies to influence what they do.

Japan's overseas investment is huge and is growing every year. Much of it is made by giant firms like Mitsubishi and Matsushita. Today, approximately 70 percent goes to North America and Europe, with the United States and the U.K. being the main targets. By setting up branch factories in these countries, Japanese firms can produce goods locally rather than **exporting** them from Japan. This means they cut down on transportation costs and customs duties. It is important to remember that far more of Japanese overseas investment has to do with services than with manufacturing.

Aid

Aid is the third overseas economic link. Japan is proud of its record of giving aid. It gives 0.3 percent of its **gross national product (GNP)**. Some goes to organizations like the United Nations; the rest goes directly to more than 130 countries, mainly in Asia, with China, Indonesia, the Philippines, and Thailand receiving the most. This direct aid takes two forms:

- grants of money and technical help from Japan
- loans for major projects, such as transportation improvements.

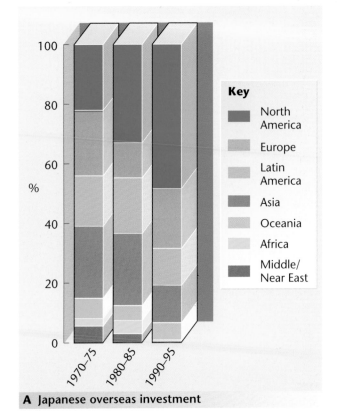

A Japanese overseas investment

Key
- North America
- Europe
- Latin America
- Asia
- Oceania
- Africa
- Middle/Near East

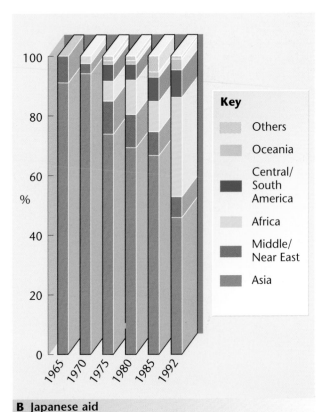

B Japanese aid

Key
- Others
- Oceania
- Central/South America
- Africa
- Middle/Near East
- Asia

AID TO CHINA

In 1995, China received 15 percent of Japan's direct aid, more than any other country. The aid was worth $1.5 billion in U.S. dollars, much of it in the form of loans. The aid is being used to help complete major projects, including new ports, **hydroelectric power** stations, a modern communications network, modernized factories, and new oil and coalfields.

Why does Japan give aid to China? Why should a small **capitalist** country be helping a huge **communist** one? Japan needs a good relationship with China because Japan is China's biggest foreign investor, and China is now Japan's second most important trading partner. Japan needs access to China's oil and coal supplies. Japan also wants to be able to sell goods to China's millions of consumers. So both Japan and China gain from the aid.

Over half of direct aid is in the form of loans from Japan. The problem is that loans have to be repaid, and interest is charged on them. Loans can easily drive poorer countries into debt.

Aid can help countries improve people's quality of life. But some projects are useful for Japanese companies too, like the building of a new port or railway line. These projects could be seen as helping Japanese companies exploit new sources of energy or raw materials, as well as helping local people.

C Japan funds major aid projects like this one in China.

FACT FILE

Overseas investment and aid: some international comparisons

	Overseas investment (U.S.$ million)		Aid	
	Outward	Inward	Total (U.S.$ million)	Ratio to GNP (%)
Japan	259.8	16.9	13,240	0.29
France	167.1	130.3	8,450	0.64
Germany	184.7	123.5	6,750	0.33
U.K.	258.7	196.3	3,090	0.30
U.S.	548.6	445.3	9,850	0.15

Overseas investment in Japan	% of all investment
United States	40.4
Netherlands	8.2
Switzerland	6.3
Germany	5.5
Canada	4.8
U.K.	4.5
Hong Kong	2.1

Economic Links between Japan and the U.S.

> ▶ **Why has Japan invested in the United States?**
> ▶ **Has it benefited the United States?**

Japan does more business with the United States than with any other country. There are two main economic links—trade and investment.

Trade

People in the United States are very aware that many household goods are made by Japanese companies, including Sony, Mitsubishi, and Nissan. But Japanese goods in the stores are just examples of trade between the two countries. Goods like Levi's Jeans and CDs by US bands are bought by Japan's wealthy and fashion-loving consumers.

Trade between Japan and the United States has winners and losers. The United States loses out on trade in goods; Japan's **exports** to the U.S. are twice as valuable as the goods the United States exports to Japan. But the United States wins on other trade, like tourism and services.

A Japanese factories are now found around the world.

Overall, the losses and gains roughly balance out. But because trade in goods is much more obvious, some people believe the United States should cut **imports** from Japan.

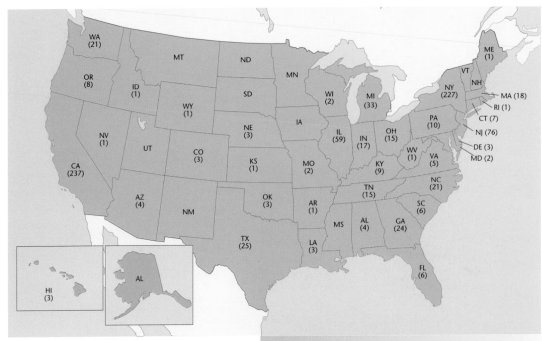

B Number of Japanese factories in the United States.

Investment in manufacturing

The U.S. and Japan have traded goods and services since 1858. Today, there are about 1,000 Japanese factories in the U.S. Trade between the U.S. and Japan is 40 percent of total world trade, and is worth over $233 billion per year. Branch factories have been set up to make goods locally, rather than importing them from Japan. There are several advantages for Japanese firms:

• They make the trade figures with Japan look better (trade friction is reduced).
• They save on transportation costs.
• They provide jobs for thousands of U.S. citizens.

Japanese factories in the U.S. make a wide range of consumer goods. Besides cars and electronics, they make things like clothes, medicines, food, and drinks. The distribution of Japanese factories in the U.S. is uneven. Most have been set up in California and New York.

Investment in services

Japanese people are great savers and investors. Recently, they have put large sums of money into banks, property, and other investments in the U.S. In return, during the past ten years, U.S. investment in Japan has increased fivefold. Japan has more invested in the U.S. than in any other country, and is the fourth largest recipient of U.S. investments.

	Goods (U.S.$ million)
U.S imports of Japanese merchandise	121
U.S exports to Japan	57

D Japanese exports and imports for the U.S.

FACT FILE

Japanese investments in U.S. industry	
Industry	**Share (%)**
Manufacturing	30.0
Construction	1.0
Commerce	13.1
Finance	15.9
Services	11.2
Transportation	0.4
Real Estate	23.1
Resources	1.8
Misc.	3.5

Grants and **incentives**
Near to parts and related industries
Low wages
Skilled workforce
Good **infrastructure**
English spoken
Other Japanese companies nearby
Friendliness
Good public order
Good domestic market

0 10 20 30 40 50 60
Number of responses

C Reasons for setting up factories in the U.S.

Japan and the Environment

▶ What has Japan achieved at home?
▶ How has its economic growth affected the global environment?

Achievements at home

Japan has done much to reduce pollution and improve the quality of the environment. The Japanese people are now much more aware of the need to protect and conserve habitats and wildlife. But there are still some problems to be solved. These include

- reducing damage to habitats caused by land **reclamation**
- finding good ways of disposing of garbage, since recycling can do only so much
- improving the design of urban environments
- imposing even tighter controls on exhaust emissions from motor vehicles.

The global environment

Since Japan's economy has become international, Japan's economic growth has affected environments outside the country.

JAPAN AND THE SEA

Japan has been reluctant to observe the international ban on commercial whaling. Whale meat has always been a delicacy in Japan, and it still appears on shop counters in Tokyo. How?

Japan's fishing fleets operate in the international waters of all the oceans. Accusations are often made about their methods and equipment—for example, the size of their nets and the fineness of the nets' mesh. Is Japan really concerned about conservation of the global fish supply?

A Japanese fleets continue to hunt whales.

JAPAN AND THE TROPICAL RAINFOREST

Japan is the world's largest consumer of tropical hardwoods. Japan **imports** tropical timber from Brazil and Southeast Asia, especially Thailand, the Philippines, Indonesia, Malaysia, and Cambodia. Japan consumes huge quantities of softwoods from Siberia and North America. But Japan has hardwoods and softwoods of its own. Why is it not harvesting these instead of felling other people's forests? Better still, why is it not using its modern technology to come up with alternative materials?

B This timber from the Malaysian rainforest has been imported to Japan.

EXPORTING POLLUTION?

Japanese overseas investment and aid have helped to set up industrial projects in developing countries. Some projects involve the refining and smelting of metal ores, as in Brazil and Indonesia. Is it just coincidence that these industries were among the worst polluters of Japan's environment during the 1960s? They are now subject to very strong antipollution control in Japan. Another example is nuclear waste, which Japan ships to Great Britain for reprocessing. So it is possible that Japan "exports" its pollution through these projects.

C This metal smelter is at Carajas in Brazil.

ACID RAIN FROM CHINA

As an economic boom sweeps across China, Chinese factories are producing record levels of pollution. In 1995, Japanese scientists reported that the area of Japan affected by **acid rain** from Chinese factories had increased by 7.5 times in two years. Over 108,000 square mi. (280,000 square km) had been damaged by the pollution.

Government officials from Japan and China have met to find ways of dealing with the problem. One solution offered by the Japanese is to build an environmental research center in Beijing. At a local level, Kitakyushu, once famous as the most polluted city in Japan, has received government aid to help the Chinese city of Dairen to improve its environment.

In 1996, the Environmental Agency reported that the level of nitrogen dioxide in the air over Japan was the highest in ten years. It also warned that the **ozone layer** over Hokkaido had decreased by 30 percent in some places. The cause of this destruction was traced to clouds of nitric acid in the air—clouds many claim originated in China.

Maybe Japan is guilty of not doing enough to ensure a sustainable use of the world's resources. Like most nations, it could also do more to protect the global environment. In either case, taking action is more effective than just talking. But there are also examples where Japan is the victim of the carelessness of other nations. When it comes to pollution, the fact is that no country stands alone.

FACT FILE

Who is responsible for the environment?
Japan's official environmental organization is the Environmental Agency, set up in 1971. Because it is an agency of the prime minister's office rather than a formal ministry, it lacks status and influence. Its two main tasks are pollution control and nature conservation.

Compared with many other countries, Japan's membership of nongovernment organizations is small, especially its branches of western-style pressure groups, such as Friends of the Earth, Greenpeace, or the World Wide Fund for Nature. The Japanese preference for cooperation rather than confrontation may be part of the reason.

However, the Japanese have shown keen and active support for local environmental programs, such as recycling garbage, cleaning up rivers, or setting up small nature reserves.

Overseas, the Japanese government is eager to take the lead in high-profile events such as the 1992 UN Conference on Environment and Development—the "Earth Summit," as it has been called. Part of Japan's aid program provides loans for pollution control and for treating environmental damage. However, it is Japan's consumer demands for fish, timber, and other environmental products that continue to threaten the global environment.

▶ What is the future for Japan and the Asian Pacific region?

As the twenty-first century begins, all nations are thinking more than usual about their futures. In Japan there are three sorts of issues to think about:

- those that are about the situation inside Japan;
- those that are about Japan and its relationships with other countries, particularly in the Asian Pacific region;
- those that are about Japan and the Asian Pacific region as a whole.

ISSUES IN JAPAN

1   The Japanese people have come to expect rising wealth and prosperity. But can an economy that has moved offshore and is based more on services keep producing more wealth?

2   Can Japan provide the services and support needed for its aging population?

3   What can be done to improve housing, the environment, and the quality of life?

4   Will Japan's **core** region continue to grow at the expense of the **periphery?**

5   Japan is already an economic superstar. Should it become more of a world political leader?

JAPAN AND THE ASIAN PACIFIC REGION AS A WHOLE

1   Should Japan speak up more in the politics of the region?

2   Would Japan benefit from setting up a free trade area in the Asian Pacific region perhaps like the European Union?

3   Would it be useful to set up a free trade area right around the Pacific Ocean?

JAPAN AND THE COMMUNIST COUNTRIES

1   Should political differences stop Japan from cooperating with these countries?

2   Can Japan encourage their economies to become more **capitalist** and market–oriented?

3   How good are the economic opportunities in these countries? Should Japan try to exploit them?

4   Will China replace Japan as the number one economy of the Asian Pacific region, and when?

JAPAN AND THE ASIAN TIGERS

1   How can Japan fight off competition from these countries?

2   Will they overtake Japan as regional leaders?

3   Can Japan cooperate more with them in investment, research, and development?

4   Should Japan be doing more to support Taiwan and South Korea? Remember that China still claims Taiwan, and there is continuing hostility between South and North Korea.

5   Will Hong Kong still be in competition with Japan now that it has returned to Chinese rule?

JAPAN AND THE LOWER-MIDDLE-INCOME ECONOMIES

1   Should Japan do more to help development in these countries?

2   Should Japan change the type of aid, shifting the emphasis from loans to grants and the transfer of technology?

3   How can Japan ensure that it uses resources from these countries in a sustainable way?

4   These countries have low wages, raw materials, and energy resources. What sort of competition could they be for Japan, and how soon?

5   Could there be more partnership between Japan and these countries?

FACT FILE

Defense
The Peace Treaty of 1951 and the Japanese constitution do not allow Japan to threaten or use military force to settle international disputes. The international community that drew up the constitution was determined that Japan should never again become a military power. Since the end of the Second World War, much of Japan's defense has been provided by the United States, which has been eager to protect Japan from invasion by **communist** troops from China or the former Soviet Union. Japan's strategic location as a base for stopping the spread of communism was also too valuable to lose.

Japan is now allowed a self-defense force that includes 1,180 tanks, 61 destroyers, and 289 fighter planes. For the last twenty years, the Japanese have limited their spending on this self-defense force to about one percent of their **GNP**—much lower than in most countries.

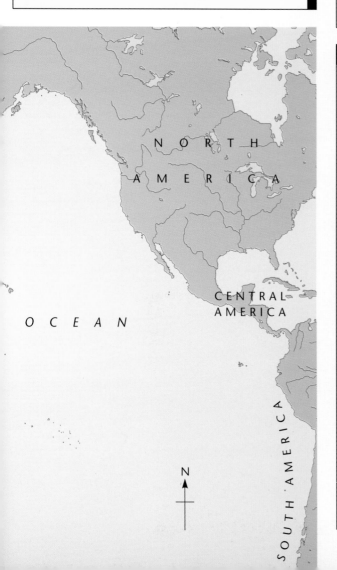

Map of Japan

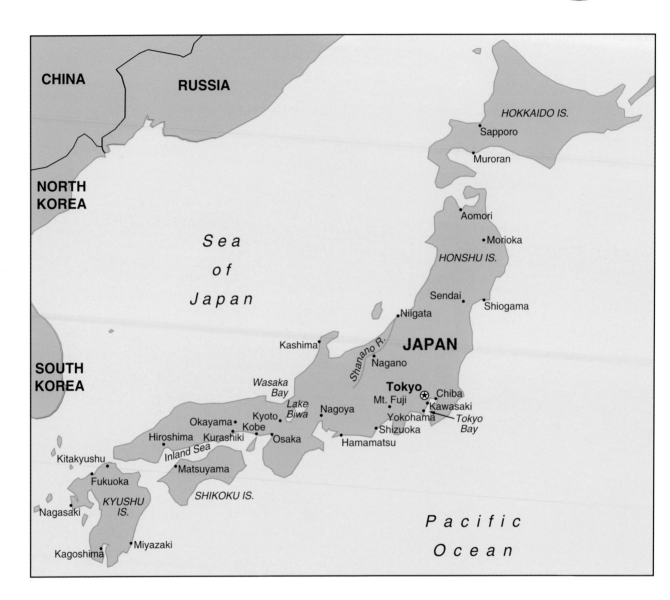

More Books to Read

Downer, Lesley. *Japan.* Austin, Tex.: Raintree Steck-Vaughn, 1995.

Heinrichs, Ann. *Japan.* Danbury, Con.: Children's Press, 1998.

Lerner Geography Department. *Japan.* Minneapolis, Minn.: Lerner Publishing Group, 1994.

Omotani, Les M. *Konnichi Wa, Japan.* Lincolnwood, Ill.: NTC Contemporary Publishing Company, 1995.

Ross, Stewart. *Rise of Japan and the Pacific Rim.* Austin, Tex.: Raintree Steck-Vaughn Publishers, 1995.

Shelley, R. *Japan.* Tarrytown, N.Y.: Benchmark Books, 1994.

Stefoff, Rebecca. *Japan.* Broomall, Penn.: Chelsea House Publishers, 1998.

Whyte, Harlinah. *Japan.* Milwaukee, Wis.: Gareth Stevens Publishing, 1999.

Glossary

accessibility how easily a place may be reached

acid rain rain with a low pH level that can be harmful to plants and animals

arable suitable for growing crops

archipelago group of islands

balance of trade difference between the value of goods exported and the value of goods imported

biotechnology technology based on biology rather than physics, such as genetic engineering

birth rate number of births in a year for every 1,000 people in a place

branch plant factory or office set up by a company because of increased business, often located far from the main factory or headquarters, perhaps overseas

bullet train high-speed train, called *shinkansen* in Japan

capitalist based on private enterprise; run by individuals rather than the government or state

communist run by the state, as an economy or society

commute to travel daily to and from work

continental climate climate that is hot in summer, cold in winter, and generally dry, usually found inland in large landmasses in the middle latitudes

cooperative group sharing equipment and acting together, like farmers when buying supplies and selling produce

core area of concentrated economic activity and development

death rate number of deaths in a year for every 1,000 people in a place

decentralization outward movement of people, jobs, and services away from core areas

demographic transition simplified way of describing how the changes in birth and death rates over time affect the total number of people in a country

dormant inactive but not dead; usually describes a volcano

export good or service sold by one country to another

face character and behavior of a person as seen by others

focus place under the ground where an earthquake starts

fold mountain part of an upland area formed by the buckling of the earth's crust

foreign aid money, technical expertise, or food that is given by one country to another country to help them with problems

free trade trading between countries without taxes, barriers, or subsidies

geothermal energy energy extracted from the earth's natural heat, such as from hot springs and certain kinds of rock

gross domestic product (GDP) total value of goods produced and services provided in a nation during one year

gross national product (GNP) GDP of a nation, plus any money earned from overseas investment and minus any money paid to people from overseas

high-tech making use of the latest technology

humid subtropical climate warm and moist climate found in areas just outside the tropics

hydroelectric power (HEP) energy produced by using the power of running water to turn generators

hydrograph graph that shows the changes in a river's flow over time

import good or service bought by one country from another

incentive encouragement or reward given for doing something

infrastructure range of services, such as communications, roads, electricity, and water supply, that is needed for economic development to take place

irrigation watering the land by artificial means, such as sprinklers, channels, etc.

island arc line of islands

joint venture business partnership in which two companies agree to share things such as research, production, management, and marketing

levee natural or artificially raised bank along the side of a river that helps hold back flood water

life expectancy average number of years a person may expect to live

market economy economy in which private individuals or companies can carry out their business with little intervention by the government

megalopolis large urban area created by the growing together of metropolitan areas and cities that were once separate

migration movement of people from one place to another

multiplier effect way in which economic growth and success in an area can attract and encourage more growth and development

natural hazard natural event, such as a volcanic eruption or flood, that threatens or causes damage to people and settlements

natural increase population growth as a result of the number of births being greater than the number of deaths

oil crisis time in 1973 and again in 1979 when the oil-producing countries raised the price of oil, causing problems for countries that depended upon its use

ozone layer part of the atmosphere that absorbs most of the harmful radiation from the sun

periphery area that falls below the level of economic development and standard of living found in the core area

plate boundary edge of a tectonic plate, or where two plates come together

polar front atmospheric condition involving warm tropical air meeting colder air from the polar regions

population density number of people living in a specific unit of area, such as people per square mile

population distribution pattern in which people are spread out across an area

precipitation moisture in the atmosphere that falls to the ground as rain, hail, snow, or sleet

prefecture Japanese equivalent of an American state; an important unit in the government of Japan

primary sector part of the economy involved in farming, fishing, forestry, and mining

public service service needed by settlements, such as water supply, sewage treatment, or public transportation

reclamation creation of new land by draining marshes, lakes, and shallow parts of the sea

Richter scale scale used to measure the magnitude of earthquakes

secondary sector part of the economy involved in manufacturing

subsidy money paid, usually by governments, to help keep a business or farm running

superpower large country with a very big population and great military power, allowing it to control or influence other countries

tectonic plate large section of the earth's crust that moves around on the heavier, liquid rock below

terrace step cut into a hillside to provide a flat area of land for farming and to control erosion

tertiary sector part of the economy involved in selling goods and providing services

trade friction bad feelings created when the trade between two countries is unbalanced; it is particularly felt by the nation with the unfavorable balance of trade

tsunami large tidal wave created by earthquake tremors, capable of causing much damage and destruction in coastal areas

typhoon tropical revolving storm with very high winds and torrential rainfall

urbanization increase and growth of towns and urban areas

Index